COVENANT • BIBLE • STUDIES

Holy War or Just Peace?
Voices from Joshua, Judges, and Ruth

Robert W. Neff
Frank Ramirez

faithQuest® ◆ Brethren Press®

Holy War or Just Peace?
Voices from Joshua, Judges, and Ruth
Covenant Bible Studies Series

© 2012 *faithQuest*®. Published by Brethren Press®, 1451 Dundee Avenue, Elgin, IL 60120. For publishing information, visit www.brethrenpress.com.

Unless otherwise noted, scripture quotations are from the New Revised Standard Version of the Bible, © 1989 National Council of the Churches of Christ in the United States of America. Used by permission. All rights reserved.

Library of Congress Cataloging-in-Publication Data

Neff, Robert W.
    Holy war or just peace? : voices from Joshua, Judges, and Ruth / Robert W. Neff, Frank Ramirez.
        p. cm.
    Summary: "Provides Bible study on themes of war and peace in the Old Testament books of Joshua, Judges, and Ruth for use in a small group setting"—Provided by publisher.
    Includes bibliographical references (p.   ) and index.
    ISBN 978-0-87178-178-9 (alk. paper)
    1. Bible. O.T. Joshua—Textbooks. 2. Bible. O.T. Judges—Textbooks. 3. Bible. O.T. Ruth—Textbooks. 4. War—Biblical teaching—Textbooks. 5. Peace—Biblical teaching—Textbooks. I. Ramirez, Frank, 1954- II. Title.

BS1295.55.N44 2012
222'.20071—dc23

                                                           2012013659

16 15 14 13 12   1 2 3 4 5

Manufactured in the United States of America

Contents

Foreword vii

Preface ix

1. The Promise and Desire for Land 1

2. Rahab and Jericho 9

3. Left-handed Ehud and His Sword 17

4. Deborah and Jael Lead the Lowly 25

5. Gideon: A Fearful Leader in a Time of Crisis 33

6. Jotham's Fable and Abimelech's Design for Kingship . .41

7. Ammonite Aggression and the Desire for More Land . . .47

8. Obedience and the Story of Samson 55

9. The Consequences of Violence 63

10. The Alternative Story of Ruth 71

Resource Pages 78

Bibliography 82

Foreword

The Covenant Bible Studies series provides *relational* Bible studies for people who want to study the Bible in small groups rather than alone.

Relational Bible study is marked by certain characteristics that differ from other types of Bible study. We are reminded that relational Bible study is anchored in covenantal history. God covenanted with people in Old Testament history, established a new covenant in Jesus Christ, and covenants with the church today. Thus, this Bible study is intended for small groups of people who can meet face-to-face on a regular basis and share frankly and covenant with one another in an intimate group.

Relational Bible study takes seriously a corporate faith. As each person contributes to study, prayer, and work, the group becomes the real body of Christ. Each one's contribution is needed and important. "For just as the body is one and has many members, and all the members of the body, though many, are one body, so it is with Christ. . . . Now you are the body of Christ and individually members of it" (1 Cor. 12:12, 27).

Relational Bible study helps both individuals and the group claim the promise of the Spirit and the working of the Spirit. As one person testified, "In our commitment to one another and in our sharing, something happened. . . . We were woven together in love by the Master Weaver. It is something that can happen only when two or three or seven are gathered in God's name, and we know the promise of God's presence in our lives."

In a small group environment, members aid one another in seeking to become:

- biblically informed so they better understand the revelation of God;
- globally aware so they know themselves to be better connected with all of God's world; and

- relationally sensitive to God, self, and others.

For people who choose to use this study in a small group, the following intentions will help create an atmosphere in which support will grow and faith will deepen.

1. As a small group of learners, we gather around God's word to discern its meaning for today.
2. The words, stories, and admonitions we find in scripture come alive for today, challenging and renewing us.
3. All people are learners and all are leaders.
4. Each person will contribute to the study, sharing the meaning found in the scripture and helping bring meaning to others.
5. We recognize each other's vulnerability as we share out of our own experience, and in sharing we learn to trust others and to be trustworthy.

The questions in the "Suggestions for Sharing and Prayer" section are intended for use in the hour preceding the Bible study to foster intimacy in the covenant group and to relate personal sharing to the Bible study topic, preparing one another to go out again in all directions to be in the world.

Welcome to this study. As you search the scriptures, may you also search yourself. May God's voice and guidance and the love and encouragement of brothers and sisters in Christ challenge you to live more fully the abundant life God promises.

Preface

On a recent visit to Paris, I went to the Carnavalet Museum, which features a whole wing on the French Revolution and the overthrow of the repressive regime of King Louis XVI and the nobles. Without making a direct historical comparison to the time of the conquest of Canaan, this period reflects a desire on the part of the poor to remove oppressive power. The symbol of this repressive power was the Bastille, the huge prison that housed political prisoners. The destruction of this structure marked the beginning of the French Revolution.

One picture that drew my attention was a painting by Hubert Robert depicting the beginning of the collapse of the Bastille; the fortress fills the entire canvas. In this painting you can see at the top of the dominant structure what looks like ants. Upon closer observation it becomes clear that the "ants" are actually people beginning the dismantling of the huge prison. When you walk into Bastille Square today, not one brick or fragment remains from the prison. Bastille Day, celebrated every July 14, is like our Fourth of July. Yet the structure that marked the beginning of the revolution is nowhere to be found.

As I thought of this Bible study, this painting of the Bastille lingered in my mind. Remnants of the city of Jericho from the time of the conquest, even its imposing walls, simply do not exist. Archaeologists are puzzled by what happened to this layer of settlement. Just like the Bastille, there are no fragments left. The outcome of the conquest is not in doubt; yet its single most imposing symbol is missing. The book of Joshua focuses on the destruction of Jericho as a pivotal part of the conquest; the historical foundation for this crucial event in the life of Israel is nowhere to be found.

The small and unrecognizable people in the painting who rebelled against what the Bastille represented succeeded in removing the government that had brought them to their knees and to starvation. Judges is a series of stories about the little people who brought an end to the repressive city-states that taxed and stole from the defenseless Israelites in the land of Canaan. These little people are represented by Ehud, who had a disability; Jael, a slave girl; Gideon, a small-town boy without status; Jephthah, a social outcast; and Samson, a playboy. These stories, unlike those in Joshua, feature the activities of "small" individuals empowered by God to bring an end to the oppressive powers.

There is a third part to the painting—a group of people who stand in the foreground, looking on, outside the inner turmoil of the revolution. In a way, they represent the people found in the book of Ruth, people from the same period but who remain outside the struggles of Joshua and Judges. These people manage to provide a just society without violence and work within a world where an alien can provide the most obedient relationship to the law. Ruth demonstrates that a just society can exist without strong people who assume control.

Frank's and my task is to provide an avenue for hearing all the voices of this period and to deal with the question of violence from all sides. The most difficult texts for believers in the historic peace church tradition, to which we belong, are found in Joshua and Judges. They give voice to a response that we do not expect. We thought we should look closer at these texts so that the complexity of the issue of violence would not be overlooked.

We wrote this study in the context of the Arab Spring, a wave of protests and civil uprisings through much of the Middle East that energized oppressed people looking for a just society. They acted in response to the accumulation of wealth in the hands of rulers—some of whom hid billions of dollars for their own interests, rather than looking to the interests of their societies.

As a nation, we recently celebrated the tenth anniversary of the terrorist attacks on September 11, 2001. After a decade, questions about the way we responded—with the invasion of a country that had nothing to do with the terror attacks, the use of torture and permanent detention of captives, as well as the loss of some civil liberties here at home—are still not resolved. How should we think about acts of violence against citizens of our own country? The books of Joshua, Judges, and Ruth seem to suggest there are several alternatives that invite—or demand— active interpretation and discussion.

Robert W. Neff
State College, Pennsylvania

Consider buying a new or used copy of *Ethnic Conflict and Civic Life: Hindus and Muslims in India* by Ashutosh Varshney. The book, which is quite readable, discusses strategies by which antagonistic cultures can live together without violence. It would make an excellent resource to guide the leader during the discussions in weeks ahead. There is a review adapted from the Second Mile Curriculum in the "Resource Pages" section at the end of this book, which will give some helpful information if you cannot obtain a copy of the Varshney book.

Frank Ramirez
Everett, Pennsylvania

1

The Promise and Desire for Land
Joshua 1 and 11

Personal Preparation

1. Read Joshua 1 and 11.
2. Acquire a copy of a reference such as *The New Interpreter's Dictionary of the Bible* for use in future sessions. Research the biblical concept of "holy war." Several denominations have worked on a statement about "just peace" for the World Council of Churches. Contact the WCC or your denominational office to obtain a copy of this statement.
3. Find the music and words for the spiritual, "When Israel was in Egypt's land," sometimes known as "Let my people go." If you are the leader of the study group, bring sheet music or download a digital version to sing along with.
4. Clip or print out a news story about oppression and struggle. How do you understand God's role in these events? How do different people in these conflicts understand what is going on? Bring your article and your musings to class.

Suggestions for Sharing and Prayer

1. Take time to meet and greet each other, welcoming new members to the group. Exchange news about what is happening in individual lives. Briefly discuss expectations, fears, and hopes for this class. The leader may then lead the group in a short time of meditative prayer.

2. These sessions deal with the identification of faith people with those who have suffered under oppression. Each week will include a different African-American spiritual to be sung by the group. Lead the group in singing "When Israel was in Egypt's land." There is no one correct version of a spiritual, so allow for differences in versions that are unearthed. Don't rush, but take time to learn and enjoy the song.

3. Read the scriptures out loud, taking turns among members of the group. Discuss your initial reaction to the stories. Discuss the definitions of "holy war" you found. How does this scripture text fit within the definition as you understand it? Share whatever versions of a statement on "just peace" you have acquired. Once again, discuss these texts in that light.

4. Share the stories you brought about oppression in various parts of the world. Discuss these matters in light of your reading of this chapter, as well as from your own biblical perspective. Make a list (and if possible, write it out on a chalkboard or newsprint) of people around the world that your group believes are suffering from oppression today.

5. Lift up these people in a series of one-sentence prayers, singing the line, "Let my people go," from the spiritual after each prayer. Conclude this time of prayer by singing the song in its entirety again.

Understanding

The first five books of the Hebrew Bible, known as the Torah or the Law, tell about a nomadic people who journey for many years without ever finding rest. They live with the promise of land given to Abraham (see Genesis 12). Joshua, the first book after the Torah, begins with the end of this journey and its culmination in the crossing of the Jordan and the entry into the land of Canaan.

After centuries of wandering, this promise appears to be fulfilled in the span of just eleven chapters. "So Joshua took the whole land . . . . And the land had rest from war" (Joshua 11:23). The goal, of course, is to bring to conclusion the ceaseless quest for a home that Israel could call its own. In Deuteronomy, the word for "rest" carries a sense of salvation; here it implies the cessation of all outside distractions and the ability to live in peace. The land is central to Israel's self-understanding and is understood as God's gift. In one of Israel's earliest confessions, we find the declaration: "[God] brought us into this place and gave us this land, a land flowing with milk and honey" (Deut. 26:9).

While the confession is clear about the source of the gift, there are a variety of confessions as to how it all came about. What we will discover are many voices and outlooks that reflect a tumultuous time that is only summarized here. Compared to the swift and orderly conquest described in Joshua, the book of Judges suggests a less than unified Israel. The conquest comes through the deception of a number of rather remarkable individuals, who unlike Joshua have little standing within the community. In contrast with them both, the book of Ruth describes an idyllic community in which Israelites and Moabites live in peace without any thought of conflict.

The Issue of Violence
The images in Joshua, such as when the walls of Jericho come tumbling down, are iconic. Even so, some Christians are uncomfortable with the way the "conquest" of the land appears to require the taking of many innocent lives. I struggle with the nature of a God who requires the death of the inhabitants of Jericho. As we will see in our discussion of Joshua 2 and 6, the requirement of the complete destruction is overruled by the confession and action of one woman, Rahab. In other words, we are not the first to ask these questions; they are there from the beginning. A critical reading of the text requires dialogue that has its origin in the text itself.

For example, in Joshua 11, Israel is under attack by the well-armed forces of the city-states that control the destinies of people in the region. These oppressors wield advanced weaponry, like the horse-drawn chariot. In a recent monograph, *Divine Presence Amid Violence*, Walter Brueggemann examines Joshua 11 and shows that the only direct word from God in this entire passage is verse 6: "And the LORD said to Joshua, 'Do not be afraid of them, for tomorrow at this time I will hand over all of them, slain, to Israel; you shall hamstring their horses, and burn their chariots with fire.'" The violence is directed against the chariots, which represented an advanced combat technology. And this is exactly what Joshua did as reported in verse 9. "This disclosure is that Yahweh gave permission for Joshua and Israel to act for their justice and liberation against an oppressive adversary. This revelation of Yahweh, given directly without conduit or process, is only authorization for a liberating movement— which is sure to be violent, but only violent against weapons" (23). It is not innocent people, but a dominating power that is dethroned by the authorizing power of God (25).

This view would seem to be substantiated by Joshua 12, where the defeated kings are listed. The final chapter before the distribution of the land does not name the native peoples. In fact, the defeats rendered in this chapter are against the kings and not their subjects. Just like the victory at the Red Sea where Pharaoh and his armies are defeated in the sea, so oppressive powers are defeated in the land. The city-states outlined in chapter 12 were often in league with Egyptian power. Just as Pharaoh enslaves the Hebrews in Egypt, we find similar enslavement in Canaan. Oppressive powers take the possessions of would-be settlers and keep them under their thumb. What is portrayed in these narratives is imperial power and its demise.

Learn Your Lessons Well

We might expect that Joshua, the new military leader, would be handed a military manual. That is not the case. Instead he is handed a law book, which will define the character of his life. This text recalls the teaching of Deuteronomy 17 on the nature of kingship. The king is to avoid symbols of power, like the acquisition of horses or the taking of many wives. He is not to elevate himself above his subjects but to spend time reading God's law. Joshua is reminded of this model of leadership when he is told: "This book of the law shall not depart out of your mouth; you shall meditate on it day and night, so that you may be careful to act in accordance with all that is written in it. For then you shall make your way prosperous, and then you shall be successful" (1:8).

Serious study remakes us in the image of what we study—in this case, the guidance that God offers us in the Word. Law is not the stick that directs us but that which infuses our whole way of being in the world. One who meditates will act naturally and speak with the force of conviction. The activity itself is such that, in the words of Jeremiah, it becomes written on the heart (31:31-34).

The Hebrew word *hagah*, translated "meditate," is not the quiet activity we normally associate with meditation. Remember that in the ancient world there was no such thing as silent reading. All reading was out loud. Depending on the context, the word *hagah* can refer to the growling of a lion (Isaiah 31:4) or the cooing of doves (Isaiah 59:11). Such vocalization suggests muttering, speaking in undertones, making the words of the law come alive in speech. So the instruction to Joshua to meditate implies speaking *and* acting. Study does imply passivity, but it involves the internalizing of what is read so that behavior will follow accordingly. This style of study is called active reading.

The result of such study is prosperity. This concept is elaborated in two biblical passages. In Psalm 1, where a similar reflection on the law occurs, prosperity implies fruitfulness. The one who meditates is like a tree that does not wither. Such words echo Psalm 92, where the righteous one flourishes like a palm tree planted in the household of God that produces fruit its whole life and remains fresh and green even as it ages. The palm tree flourishes in all kinds of weather, because it is not dependent upon external circumstances but draws water from artesian wells far below the surface of the desert. No matter what happens around the oasis, the palm tree still produces fruit. To be planted, in this case in God's Word, provides nourishment in any and all circumstances, including times of stability as well as times of great change and transition (as is the case in Joshua 1).

The second theme of this section is: "Be strong and courageous; do not be frightened or dismayed" (1:9). But what is the source of this serenity that Joshua is meant to attain? It does not depend upon what is happening around him. After all, the great leader Moses has died. The people are moving into new and hostile territory. The land is filled with walled cities and armed populations. This new inexperienced leader requires reassurance, which will come through the constant reminder that the source of his strength is daily meditation on the law of God.

Huston Smith, the great religious historian, recalls the image of his father, a Christian missionary, at the time of the Cultural Revolution in China. There were unbelievable threats and challenges. What surprised Smith was the utter serenity of this father who faced cruel pressures and certain loss. Yet he did not vary from his routine and study, and it was from this daily devotion that he found strength to face the rising uncertainty. The same priority lies in the activity and behavior of Joshua as he leads his people into the land promised to them.

Discussion and Action

1. Joshua is told three times in chapter 1 to be strong and courageous. How do you react when someone repeats instructions to you several times in a row? Do you feel trusted? Affirmed? Are you annoyed? What value is there to encouragement? Are you an encourager?

2. Joshua is told to keep God's Word before him. How hard do you find it to make the study of God's Word and prayer a regular part of your day? What gets in the way, and how do you get back on track? If you have tried before and failed, what circumstances interrupted this practice?

3. What is your view of the book of Joshua? How has your opinion changed from what you might have learned as a child in Sunday school to how you now experience it as an adult? In general, what is your opinion of the Hebrew Bible? Name your most favorite and least favorite books in the Old Testament. Where do Joshua, Judges, and Ruth fit in all this?

4. Discuss the definitions of "holy war" and "just peace" that you brought to the group (see "Personal Preparation") and how they relate to Joshua 11. What are your thoughts about this account of God's gift of the land to Israel? How do you understand God's role in the giving of this gift?

5. Share your clippings or downloaded articles about current situations of oppression and struggle. What are some differing views about these situations? How does the book of Joshua speak to these situations? Do you believe God has a hand in today's politics? What role did God play in the biblical account? What role does God play now?

6. Compare the biblical concept of the land as God's gift to Israel to our own country's view of Manifest Destiny. How does this look differently to European Americans and Native Americans?

7. Discuss the definitions of "holy war" you discovered in reference works and as it appears to you in scripture. What does the author of this study say about the nature of the war? What is your opinion about this warfare?

8. What are your views on violence in scripture? When, if ever, is violence justified? How does this passage speak to your understanding of God?

2

Rahab and Jericho

Joshua 2 and 6

Personal Preparation

1. Find copies of the spirituals, "Joshua fit the battle of Jericho" and "Were you there," and bring them to the session.
2. Read Joshua 2 and 6. Write down your impressions in a single sentence. Read today's lesson, and then review your sentence. Would you change it? If so, how? Bring your sentences to the session.
3. Search for an article on Jericho and reflect on the archaeological findings at this historic site.
4. Review Deuteronomy 7:1-6, 13:12-18, and 20:1-20, which describe the basis for the ban and the rules of warfare. Look up "ban" (*cherem*) in a reference work such as *The New Interpreter's Dictionary of the Bible*. Rephrase the definition in your own words and bring it to the session.

Suggestions for Sharing and Prayer

1. Share joys and concerns, taking time in prayer for group members.
2. Share memories about the song, "Joshua fit the battle of Jericho." Sing through it, either with a leader .or by playing a digital download. Compare and contrast how you felt about the story when you were younger, and what these images associated with the fall of a city and slaughter mean to you now.

3. Focus on what the author says in this session about Rahab and her identification with a people who escaped from slavery. Imagine yourself present in this biblical narrative. Do you imagine yourself as one of the spies? As Rahab? As Rahab's family? As one of those searching for the spies? What would you say or do in such circumstances? As a group, role-play some of these characters.

4. Share some of your feelings about relating to different parts of a story. How easy do you find it to inhabit another's viewpoint? Discuss times when you found yourself on one side of a divisive issue. How willingly do you articulate the other side's position?

5. Enter into a time of open prayer for one another and for some of the topics and issues that were raised in your discussion of the previous questions. The leader should close with a benediction. Return to "Joshua fit the battle of Jericho" and sing it one more time.

Understanding

"In light of the acts of terrorism on September 11, 2001, please be advised this product contains scenes that may be considered disturbing to some viewers." So read a warning affixed for a time by one large video rental chain to movies depicting buildings falling down.

But the attitude of contrition didn't last long, and soon movies once more included scenes of buildings blowing up and collapsing in a cloud of dust. When it's not a real event, people like scenes of destruction.

Maybe that's why the song, "Joshua fit the battle of Jericho," was one of my favorites when I was young. The image of the walls tumbling down was etched in my memory. I loved the miraculous collapse of this huge walled city. I rejoiced in both the poetry and the powerful display of God's power.

Now, as an adult, I wonder which was the greater miracle: the fall of Jericho or the sparing of Rahab and her family.

There is a stunning revelation in Joshua 2 and 6: twenty-eight verses relate to Rahab and her family and only twenty-one to the fall of Jericho, of which only two relate to the actual collapse of the city walls and the *cherem* (the Hebrew word for the biblical command to destroy everything associated with a culture, including a people). Of greater interest to me is the anomaly that Rahab and her family represent. There are to be no exceptions to the *cherem*, yet Rahab and her family are spared, much like Lot and his family in Genesis 18 and 19.

As a prostitute, Rahab seems an unlikely role model, yet in the New Testament she is praised as a heroine of the faith. In Matthew 1, she is listed among the ancestors of Jesus. And in Hebrews, a whole verse is devoted to her: "By faith Rahab the prostitute did not perish with those who were disobedient, because she had received the spies in peace" (11:31). She becomes a model for the theme of the book of James: "Likewise, was not Rahab the prostitute also justified by works when she welcomed the messengers and sent them out by another road?" (2:25). Perhaps this story in Joshua is really about the deliverance of the least likely, the lowly and despised.

Why Rahab?

In Ephesus, our tour guide showed us a sign painted on the roadway. It depicted a woman's face and an arrow directing sailors to the house of prostitution in the center of the city. Unlike Ephesus, the "red light" district in Jericho was on the outskirts of the city, alongside or within the city wall.

The Hebrew spies were spotted soon after they arrived in the city. It turns out that the inhabitants of Jericho were on high alert as this large group of nomads made its way into the area outside Jericho and then into the city. Fortunately for the spies, Rahab, at great risk, concealed them and made her story believable enough that they remained undetected until they escaped.

So why would spies come to a prostitute's house, and why would Rahab risk her life and her family to conceal them? Why would a biblical story contain lies, betrayals, and feature a harlot as a heroine? And why is there a need for all of this secrecy, spying, betrayal, and risk if the miracle of Jericho is in view? These are all important questions. Some of the answers may help us better understand the conquest of the land as we find it in Joshua and Judges.

The Backstory to Our Story

A good actor knows a lot about the background and history of the character he or she plays, stuff that is never shown on stage but that informs the character's motivation and action. This is known as the backstory. This chapter of our study has a backstory that answers a lot of questions. It is found in Exodus 5, where the Israelites are described as a slave people in Egypt, forced laborers who do menial tasks. Many scholars equate their identity with a class of people known as *'apiru* who are mentioned in nonbiblical documents of this time. These nomadic groups were enslaved in difficult times. Some suggest that this was an economic choice and a matter of survival.

That's part of the backstory. Additionally, some scholars suggest that the Hebrew Bible presents two different stories about the way the Promised Land came to be occupied by people identified with Israel. One tells of a quick conquest in Joshua, and the other in Judges occurs over a long period of time. This suggests that the success of the conquest not only depended upon God's guidance, but also on a strategy of relating to the oppressed people in the land of Canaan—all as part of God's design in freeing the slaves from the hand of Pharaoh.

If Joshua 2 is an illustration of just such a situation, suddenly the spies showing up in the home of a harlot makes perfect sense. As former slaves, they would naturally relate to one of the underclass families in the land. Then, as now, many involved in the sex trade are virtual slaves. This could also explain Rahab's cooperation with these foreigners. Perhaps it is not only her fear of God, but also her hope for a better life. There is no sexual innuendo in this story. Instead, what appears to be a clear act of treason on the part of Rahab in concealing the spies and plotting their escape, turns out to be an act of common cause and shared interests.

We are now in a position to answer the question posed earlier in this section. The story is about a household that apparently experienced oppression and slavery, much as Israel did. Their location on the edge of the city is a metaphor for a family on the fringe. Israel could and did relate to such people. The sessions on the book of Judges that follow will show how a disabled person, a slave girl, a coward, an outcast, and a clown all provide deliverance for Israel. There is an interesting parallel in the New Testament where Jesus is accused of relating to tax collectors, prostitutes, and all manner of sinners. It is a consistent biblical theme that God reaches out and claims those who are in need, those many have given up on.

This may be one of the reasons why this story is placed at the beginning of the conquest of Canaan. Rahab's story is a paradigm, or example, of how God takes the side of the oppressed against the powerful.

A Confession of Faith

Rahab is more than a bystander. She embraces the faith of Israel, as indicated by her confession of faith in 2:11, and her life is transformed. She does not continue in her profession, but marries and becomes part of the genealogy of David and Jesus.

Therefore, even though she did not experience the exodus event, she is able to embrace this delivering God. Her confession of faith provides the avenue for the addition of a whole new class of people who had not fled Egypt, but were anxious to escape the oppression of the land. Israel is defined by God's deliverance at the Red Sea (see Exodus 14 and 15), which was so well-known that even foreigners like Rahab knew all about it (Joshua 2:9-11).

The collapse of the walls of Jericho was the first step in the taking of the land. That's why American slaves claimed the story of the Israelites as their story and sang songs like "Joshua fit the battle of Jericho." They anticipated the day when the walls would come tumbling down on the oppressive system of slavery in the United States.

The deliverance from Egypt and the conquest of the land are bookends to the theme of God's deliverance from oppression.

There's the celebration of the Passover (Joshua 5) in advance of the victory, the crossing of the waters on dry ground, the miraculous vanquishing of the enemy, and the deliverance by a talisman—the red blood on the door lintel of Israelite homes in Egypt and the red thread in the window of Rahab's home in Jericho. The comparisons are meant to suggest that God continues to be the victor over oppressive powers, both in Egypt and in Canaan.

The story of the collapse of Jericho assures that the experience of outsiders, like the family of Rahab, mirrors the experience of the Israelites in Egypt. Rahab and her family can claim the same miraculous deliverance by God that was the experience of Israel at the Red Sea. The experience of God's saving power in the past became the experience of those in each successive generation. At each celebration of the Passover, these former slaves were never to forget their origins and continue to reflect on the plight of other oppressed peoples in similar circumstances. Indeed, for Jews through the centuries, celebrating Passover cements their living bond with the past, present, and future, making them a part of the story. The same is true for the Christian celebration of communion.

Discussion and Action

1. Read or sing, "Joshua fit the battle of Jericho." What walls have come tumbling down in your life, sweeping away barriers of attitude or action? What walls remain and have yet to come tumbling down?

2. The story of Jericho's fall has been used by some to justify acts of violence, and even genocide. What level of discomfort do you have with the violent aspects of this story? To what extent do you accept or reject stories such as these because they have a place in the Bible? How have you heard this story interpreted in sermons or studies?

3. Were you more or less comfortable with the story of the destruction of a city full of people when you were a child than you are as an adult? What explanations did you require as a child versus now as an adult? What is

your comfort level with stories about the taking of the land and the destruction of the inhabitants?

4. How does singing compare to telling (or hearing) a biblical account?

5. Discuss some of what you learned about the historical Jericho from Bible dictionaries and commentaries. How does this compare with what you may have learned earlier? How closely does it parallel the biblical account?

6. What are the defining moments of your congregation's history? Is your congregation's history known by all? Has it been written down, and if so, are there competing accounts of what happened? If there are stories of inclusion, similar to that of Rahab and her family, in your congregation's history, share them with your group.

7. Think of the best stories that define the life of your family or larger clan. Are they perfectly accurate in all details? What portions, if any, are exaggerated? How does this affect the story?

8. Would you prefer the biblical account to be literally accurate—including the deaths of the men, women, and children of Jericho—or a figurative story with its own truth that does not involve anyone's death?

9. What is the meaning of the ban (*cherem*) as you understand it, drawing from this session and from the definition you looked up in a reference work? Compare your understanding with others from the group.

3

Left-handed Ehud and His Sword
Judges 3

Personal Preparation

1. Read Psalms 72 and 82, and Judges 3. Write down three things that strike you about these passages. If the story of Ehud reminds you of a current story in the news, bring it to the session.
2. Look up the spiritual, "I couldn't hear nobody pray," and bring a copy to the session.
3. Define "disability." Reflect on aspects of your life and situation that might qualify as disabilities, and also on those elements that might put you ahead of others. How do these balance out?
4. How easy is it for people to get around in your church building? Is it accessible to those with physical disabilities, with mental and emotional disabilities? What barriers exist?

Suggestions for Sharing and Prayer

1. Introduce and sing, "I couldn't hear nobody pray." Emphasize the importance of everyone participating. Then pray the Lord's Prayer line by line. Invite someone to pray each line of the prayer, and after each line, pause for free prayers based on that line.
2. Share your definitions of what constitutes a disability or handicap. What sort of language should be used for various conditions? If you made a handicap accessibility

census of the facility in which you meet, share observations and remedies.

3. Read Psalms 72 and 82 aloud. Compare these different images of what it means to be a leader. Discuss times when you have been called into leadership, and share some of the frustrations, successes, and failures you experienced.
4. Enter the story of Ehud. As a group, try to put together an autobiographical narrative for Ehud, outlining the life he experienced and highlighting his frustrations and limitations.
5. The spiritual chosen for this week touches on how praying aloud strengthens other believers. What feelings do you have about praying aloud and silently? What are the strengths and weaknesses of each? Enter into a time of open prayer, and close by singing, "I couldn't hear nobody pray," changing the words if you like to, "Yeah, I hear everybody pray."

Understanding

It is said that during an especially dark moment of the Civil War someone attempted to comfort Lincoln by reminding him that God was on their side. According to the story, the president replied, "Sir, my concern is not whether God is on our side; my greatest concern is to be on God's side."

If God is on anyone's side, it is on the side of the oppressed, at least as far as the Hebrew Bible is concerned. This is a consistent theme in scripture from the exodus to the conquest. In Psalm 82, for example, there is a dramatic scene in which God sits among the gods of the nations to judge their capacity to rule. They are found wanting because they judge unjustly and favor the wicked over the weak and the orphan, the lowly and the destitute (vv. 3-4). Because they have failed in their function as gods, they are sentenced to mortality and will die (vv. 6-7).

The implication is that the true ruler reflects the divine passion for justice. In the words of Psalm 72, "He delivers the needy when they call, the poor and those who have no helper. He has pity on the weak and the needy, and saves the lives of the needy. From oppression and violence he redeems their life; and precious is their blood in his sight" (vv. 12-14). The function of the ruler is to care for those who might be overlooked or trampled upon by the more powerful.

The Hebrew Bible takes a grim view of the character of kings who have a tendency to fill their own pockets at the expense of their subjects. They fail in their God-given task over and over again. Later in this series we will examine Jotham's fable, which clearly expresses the view that those who desire to become king are the least qualified to rule. A similar view is expressed in 1 Samuel 8, where the prophet warns that a king will take all his subjects' earthly possessions to keep his own household going. In 1 Kings 12, the young king Rehoboam makes no attempt to hide his venality. Instead, he promises to gouge his subjects with even greater taxes than his father Solomon levied. Is it little wonder that the people revolt?

A similar view is found in Daniel and Esther, where foreign kingship is characterized by opulence and great wealth. These kings are easily led astray by courtiers, as in Esther, and in so doing subvert their own best interests. In the end, their fate is sealed by their failure to rule wisely. In Daniel we experience royalty so caught up in the display of power that they cannot recognize their friends, and jeopardize their own future, as well as the nation's.

King Eglon in Judges 3 provides a graphic example of this viewpoint. The Moabite king is fat and pampered, sitting in his own cool chamber as his subjects are roasting outside. This king has overindulged himself. He is easily deceived, and depends on his own analysis of the situation rather than consulting his advisors. He has a lofty view of himself and cannot believe a man like Ehud (whose impairment will be discussed below) could cause him any harm. The setting is, of course, the delivery of taxes from an oppressed people, taxes that do not aid the people through the creation of infrastructure and services, but only serve to enhance the outrageous behavior of an oversatiated king.

Moab was an established nation before Israel showed up on the scene. They used their advantage to collect tribute from the Israelites for eighteen years (v. 14). Ehud, a Benjaminite, was charged with delivering the tribute to the king. He required a group of individuals to assist in the transaction. Once the tribute was in the hands of the king, the tax obligation was met. Everyone relaxed; only Ehud stayed behind to talk with the king. Who was this man, Ehud?

Right Hand or Left Hand?

I still remember my fifth grade writing class, where if you didn't write with your right hand, you would be cracked with a ruler until you did. That was in the 1940s. My parents insisted that my sister and I use our right hands. Though I happened to be ambidextrous, I was still instructed to use my right hand.

When I took anthropology at Cambridge University in the 1970s, I became aware of the cultural roots of this practice. In traditional cultures, the right hand was used for eating, often from a communal dish. The left hand was used for body cleanliness. You can imagine the outrage if someone used their left hand at the dinner table.

In this story, the accent falls on a left-handed individual, clearly a cultural misfit in his world. The text suggests that Ehud was left-handed because of a deformity and had no other choice but to use his culturally unclean hand. This does not sound like the recipe for a great warrior.

Nor did he have much of a weapon. Ehud seems to have carried nothing more than a stick about a cubit in length (approximately 14 inches) that has been sharpened on both sides. This is not surprising. There was no metallurgy among the tribes of Israel at that time. If that is the case, we can understand why he escaped detection. I am tempted to suggest that he had nothing more than a wooden sword, much like a young boy with a toy. He carries this "weapon" on the right side, further facilitating the ruse. Right-handed people wore their swords on their left hip. Who would search someone's right hip for a weapon?

The situation is full of irony—a man from the tribe of Benjamin, which literally means "son of the right hand," representing his tribe with a deformed right hand, brings a toy weapon concealed on the wrong side of the body. Because he does not seem to be a danger, Ehud is left alone with a highly protected king. His deception works because the Moabites are blinded by their right-handed assumptions and their view of weaponry. No one suspects anything. With the approval of the king, who perhaps hoped for a bribe, the two are left alone.

A Mission from God?
What motivates Ehud? As most commentators suggest, Ehud was working on his own; he was never directed by God in the narrative to assassinate Eglon. Although he declared that he had a message from God, there is no divine word given to him in the text. When the king heard that Ehud had a message from God, he rose, conceivably out of deference, to receive the message. Ehud then slew him in one of the most horrifying scenes in the Bible. The reader is appalled at the fat and the bile engulfing the wooden sword to such an extent that it cannot be withdrawn. There's no getting around the graphic description in the text. It's disgusting! But it is there to dramatize the destiny of over-indulged and pampered leaders.

The story invites us to root for Ehud and the oppressed. His assassination plot freed God's people from Moabite rule. But should we cheer? Even in the narrative there is ambiguity about the will of God in this. There is no directive, as in the stories of Gideon, where a God-given ruse causes the enemy to self-destruct. For religious people of many traditions there are moments in history that call for direct action. But how direct? And what type of action is justified against oppression? Clearly, for Gandhi, nonviolence was the only way to overthrow British rule. Martin Luther King, Jr., insisted that nonviolence was essential to the successful civil rights movement.

But are there situations in which violence may be necessary? In the face of the atrocities perpetrated by Nazi Germany, some felt that violence was essential. In his autobiography, the commentator Andy Rooney admitted that at the start of World War II he had applied for conscientious objector status, but eventually decided he might object against violence, but he wasn't truly conscientious. Later, while serving as a journalist in the armed forces, he was present at the liberation of the concentration camps and decided that violence was the only way these horrors could be stopped.

Then there is the case of Dietrich Bonhoeffer, one of the most profound and admired theologians of the twentieth century. He became part of a plot to assassinate Hitler. He felt that as a disciple of Jesus Christ he was called to rid the world of great evil because of the great injustices of the Third Reich. The plot failed; Bonhoeffer was arrested, imprisoned, and eventually executed.

And finally, after the killing of Osama bin Laden in 2011, the Dalai Lama, while admitting he would not willingly kill a mosquito, suggested that those like bin Laden who perpetrate violent acts ought, on occasion, become the subject of violence themselves.

For a pacifist, the narrative of Ehud presents problems. Justice issues do not recede into the background for Jesus. He spoke against oppressive authority and taxation, as represented by the story of the cleansing of the temple. To my mind, at least, he shared with the Zealots, guerilla fighters in first-century Judea, a loathing for Roman disrespect of human life and their use of violence to keep the peace. Yet he chose to part ways with the Zealots when it came to the violent overthrow of the government. The key issue in the biblical story is the pursuit of justice. What does this mean for Christian behavior, even when one shuns violence as a possible solution?

Discussion and Action

1. How do Ehud's actions conform to the biblical understanding of judgeship? See Judges 2:11-23 for a better understanding of the role of judges in this context.

2. The author suggests that in the Hebrew Bible, God demands that a desire for justice be the primary motive of a good ruler. When have you seen such a desire displayed by leadership? When has it seemed lacking? In

our time, should assassination be accepted as a way to achieve justice? How do you react to this account about Ehud's actions being included in scripture? Discuss whether such plots are ever morally right, and if you see God in acts of violence, death, and destruction.

3. Ehud's actions liberate the people for a time. Do these results justify his choice of violence? Do the actions of King Eglon justify whatever violence is used against him? When are nonviolent means of resistance appropriate and effective, in your opinion?

4. How do you expect others to respond to foreign domination? Should they bear up under oppression or take action? If so, what sort of action? Do you think your response would be different if the oppression was on the other side of the world, or if it was in your own community? Explain your response.

5. In the late nineteenth century, the first automatic weapon, known as the Maxim gun, provided a temporary technological advantage for the British. As the satirist Hilaire Belloc put it: "Whatever happens, we have got / The Maxim gun, and they have not." How important is it to maintain a technological advantage in weaponry at the expense of others? How did having such an advantage help the Moabites in this story? Has a technological advantage helped the United States in its most recent military conflicts?

6. Costa Rica, in contrast to its neighbors in Central America, prides itself on having no standing army. Is this realistic? Is it possible for a large nation to exist without an army? How can nations resist evil without resorting to war?

7. Ehud is a handicap by the standards of his day. What do you and your congregation do with regard to ministry with the disabled? How welcoming to people with various kinds of disabilities are your building and your programs? Do you support groups like Special Olympics, involve yourself in fundraisers, and provide advocacy and support?

4

Deborah and Jael Lead the Lowly
Judges 4–5

Personal Preparation

1. Read Judges 4 and 5. Look for artistic depictions of this story on the Internet and bring a printout, if possible, to class.
2. Look up stories about the civil rights movement, such as those about the Freedom Riders, Rosa Parks, or Martin Luther King, Jr.
3. Research the music or obtain a digital file of "Every time I feel the Spirit."
4. Consult—and borrow if necessary—a liturgy or book of hours that provides a guide for daily responsive prayers. Bring the readings that go with it to the upcoming session.

Suggestions for Sharing and Prayer

1. Sing "Every time I feel the Spirit" a couple of times, to get to know the lyrics. Spend a little time in fellowship, speaking of whatever comes to mind.
2. Share occasions when you have had to totally trust God with regard to your circumstances. How comfortable do you feel relying on others? Relying on God? Have there been occasions when you had to go forward in faith, relying on the Spirit without a plan or the certainty of an outcome? Discuss these occasions and what you learned from them.

3. If you found artistic renderings of this story (see "Person-
    al Preparation"), share them with your group. How do
    these images match your idea of what faith is like?
4. Share with group members circumstances that may lie
    ahead for you, your family, or your church that will
    require trust in the midst of uncertainty. Discuss the
    place of God's spirit in circumstances that require trust.
    Take time to pray for an openness to trust. Pray with,
    and for, one another in turn.
5. Turn to the liturgy, book of hours, or lectionary that you
    brought to the session (see "Personal Preparation").
    Choose one person to be the leader for the responsive
    readings, and then pray together. Close by singing again,
    "Every time I feel the Spirit."

Understanding

Unlike the conquest tradition in Joshua where the indigenous
nations appear to be wiped out, the early chapters of Judges suggest that many different peoples remained in the land for many
different reasons. In Judges 1:22-26, a man of Bethel who assists
in the capture of the city is spared. Benjaminites and Jebusites
live together in Jerusalem (1:20). The Amorites and the Danites
share the same territory, one living in the plains and the other in
the hills (1:34). Judges 4 and 5 continue this story line. Jael is a
Kenite whose family has forged an alliance with Jabin, the king
of Hazor, but she does not allow this alliance to prohibit her from
joining forces with Israel, much like Rahab in Joshua 2.

Judges 4 and 5 contain some of the oldest narrative and poet-
ic material found in the Hebrew Bible. They were composed
close to the events they describe. In the backstory for our study
of Joshua 2 and 6 we looked at the Israelites in Egypt, where they
are described as *'apiru*, household slaves. In Judges 5, the people
of Israel are described differently—as peasantry (vv. 7 and 11)
who apparently made a living plundering caravans on their way
to Egypt (vv. 6-7). The word *perazon*, peasants, is used only
here, but could be the background for the Perizzites, whom we
meet in other biblical texts. The word implies that these people

lived in the open country, as opposed to those who lived in walled cities. Such a definition would fit the context of these chapters.

Even with this definition, the Israelites remain an underclass. Consider some of the startling contrasts in these two chapters between the Israelites and the forces led by Jabin. Jabin's troops have chariots of iron. Chariots are made of wood and use iron to hold them together, so the term "chariots of iron" is an exaggeration to stress the oppressive nature of Jabin's troops. They carry weapons of iron, unlike Israel who has no shield or spear (5:8). For this reason the poet writes, "My heart goes out to the commanders of Israel who offered themselves willingly among the people" (5:9). Jabin and his troops live inside walled cities, while the Israelites lived outside the walled cities. The principal figure, Jael, lived in a tent, as opposed to the more permanent homes of the rulers.

Who Is the Real Hero?
Consistent with the theme of Judges, the one who appears to be weak demonstrates the strength of God in driving away the oppressors. A woman, Deborah, is the one who takes initiative and tells the commander Barak to take a position on Mount Tabor. God has revealed that the troops of Jabin will be given into his hand. Barak demurs and says, "If you will go with me, I will go; but if you will not with me, I will not go" (4:8). These are not the words of a courageous leader, but the words of a fearful and dependent man. Some of the tribes express similar reluctance. Reuben is described as having "great searchings of heart" (5:15-16) and remained at home. Gilead stayed in the safety of the land beyond the Jordan; Dan and Asher preferred the coast and the stillness of the sea (v. 17). Judah, Levi, and Simeon are not even mentioned.

Once again it is not by the might of weapons or armies that the oppressors are overthrown. The real hero is, of course, the Lord: "LORD, when you went out from Seir, when you marched from the region of Edom, the earth trembled, and the heavens poured, the clouds indeed poured water" (5:4). It would appear that Sisera's troops self-destruct in the wake of a flash flood:

"All the army of Sisera fell by the sword; no one was left" (4:16). In the end, Barak's troops are not described as doing anything. Just like the story of Gideon in the next chapters, the Lord sets the army into a panic and a threat to Israel is removed.

As with the exodus, here the God of Israel appears as a mighty warrior defeating the forces of oppression. God appears in the wind and rains to defeat the well-organized troops of Israel's enemies. How shall we understand this activity? These narratives are part of a larger history that ends with Israel's defeat at the hands of Babylon (2 Kings 24–25 and the prophet Jeremiah, selected texts). The reason for the destruction of Jerusalem and Judah lies with God's desire for justice. Israel has been disobedient in its care for all members of its society. Rather than at some eschatological time removed from history, here God acts in the historical moment to bring about judgment in real time. God seeks justice in the thread of history. The compiler of the tradition connects disobedience in the time of the Judges, which led to oppression, with the experience of the Judeans under the Babylonians. The past is interpreted to make sense of the present.

This theme of God's judgment and call for justice is reiterated in Psalms 82, 94, and 96, and in Psalms 2 and 149, which frame the Psalter. The prophets from the eighth century to the sixth century repeatedly called for repentance, as was so eloquently stated in Micah 6:8: "What does the LORD require of you but to do justice?" In an ironic twist, Jonah calls Assyria to repent of its violence: "All shall turn from their evil ways and from the violence that is in their hands" (Jonah 3:8). In Chronicles, David is prohibited from building the temple because of the blood on his hands: "You have shed much blood and have waged great wars; you shall not build a house to my name, because you have shed so much blood in my sight on the earth" (1 Chron. 22:8). Violence is clearly an issue in the later biblical texts, but the commitment of God to justice never vanishes and remains a core of Old Testament belief. The reader is not faced with a violent warrior, but a God who sides with the oppressed in seeking justice for the lowest of society.

An Unlikely Heroine

These narratives in Judges are filled with unlikely heroes. In this story Jael, a bedouin woman, brings down the great general Sisera by using the craft that is part of her daily life. Bedouin women carry the responsibility of pitching the tent as the nomadic family moves from place to place. She would drive the tent pegs into the earth to hold the family dwelling in place, so this occasion was not the first time she used these objects.

In addition, she deceives the general. Sisera assumes that he can rely on the alliance of Jabin and her family. She offers him hospitality, as one would expect. The rule of bedouin life was to assure the safety of anyone who comes into the household. She provides a place to rest and milk to slake his thirst.

What happens next is a breach of the most fundamental rule of hospitality and the alliance forged by her family. She murders Sisera while he sleeps. The lowest brings down the lofty. What seems to be the act of a traitor (remember Rahab?) can be interpreted as the act of an oppressed person who finds common cause with Israel. A poor bedouin woman brings down the oppressor. The least likely agent becomes the avenue of freedom.

Such a theme is enunciated at the close of this period in the words of Hannah: "There is no Holy One like the LORD, no one besides you; there is no Rock like our God. . . . The bows of the mighty are broken, but the feeble gird on strength. . . . He raises up the poor from the dust; he lifts the needy from the ash heap . . . . He will guard the feet of his faithful ones, but the wicked shall be cut off in darkness; for not by might does one prevail" (1 Samuel 2:2, 4, 8*a*, 9).

The narrative exalts the lowly and brings low the high and lofty. The justice of God is real for those who are oppressed.

Discussion and Action

1. Take apart the conversation between Deborah and Barak. What kind of person do you imagine Deborah to be? How should Barak have responded? Deborah and

Jael might be described as unlikely heroes. Who are some other unlikely heroes?

2. Deborah calls upon Barak to trust in God's guidance during this crisis. Talk about a time when you did not make preparations, yet things turned out all right. Talk about a time when you did not make preparations and things did *not* turn out all right. What is the proper balance between trust and faith in tough times?

3. Jael can be accused of breaking the solemn rules about hospitality that were observed in the Middle East. What is the justification for her actions? When, if ever, have you broken a law or custom for the sake of a higher good? What were the repercussions? What is your understanding of the meaning of civil disobedience? When is it appropriate?

4. Discuss the image of God as a mighty warrior in this chapter. Is this how you experience God? If not, why not? Under what circumstances, if any, might seeing God as a warrior be helpful?

5. How do you think the will of God is accomplished as the Spirit moves among Barak, Deborah, and Jael? Discuss ways in which resolve or timidity may have aided or slowed the actions of the Spirit in your lives as individuals and as a congregation.

6. Imagine writing a news story about this biblical story. What headline would you write? What would be the opening paragraph? Who would get the most credit for what happened? What lines from this story would you quote?

7. Recall sermons, Sunday school lessons, or articles that have touched on this story. Where does this story rank in your favorite or least favorite biblical stories? Look again at the artistic renderings of this story people found. Discuss whether these are pictures you would like displayed in church hallways or in stained glass. Why, or why not?

8. Discuss ways in which what appears to be weakness in the eyes of the larger society can, in fact, be strength.
9. Close by singing again, "Every time I feel the Spirit."

5

Gideon—A Fearful Leader in a Time of Crisis
Judges 6–8

Personal Preparation

1. Read the story of Gideon in Judges 6–8. Look up the word "ephod" in a Bible dictionary or on the Internet prior to the session.
2. Look up the Hebrew word *gabor*, sometimes translated as "mighty man" or "warrior," in a Bible dictionary or commentary. How frequently does this word occur? How is it translated?
3. Research the hymn, "I am leaning on the Lord." Bring music or a digital copy to the session. Purchase or borrow crayons to bring to the "Sharing and Prayer" session.
4. Call to mind an action or a speech on the part of someone who helped deflect a potentially violent situation. Write a short paragraph about that incident and be prepared to share that during the session.

Suggestions for Sharing and Prayer

1. After a greeting and an opening prayer by the leader, sing "I am leaning on the Lord." This week's session is titled, "A Fearful Leader in a Time of Crisis." Discuss whether you are more apt to lean on God or to forget about God when crisis strikes. Share examples from

your lives. Through sentence prayers, lift up those who
may currently be going through crises.

2. Gideon's self-image seems to be fragile. He protests,
   "My clan is the weakest in Manasseh, and I am the least
   in my family" (6:15). Despite his apparent terror in this
   divine encounter, the angel greets him as a *gabor*, a
   Hebrew word meaning "mighty man." Take time now to
   address each other with positive and uplifting terms, and
   explain why you are using this term to describe the particular group member.

3. Use crayons and paper to illustrate this story. Depending
   on the number in the group, assign portions of the story
   to each person. After, put the art together to retell the
   biblical story.

4. Return to "I am leaning on the Lord." Between stanzas,
   invite each group member to make a statement about a
   way in which they commit to leaning upon God in times
   of crisis.

5. Close with a general prayer, concluding with the Lord's
   Prayer in unison.

Understanding

This is one of my favorite Old Testament stories because there
is so much irony in it. We first meet Gideon in the bottom of a
vat in the middle of a vineyard. He's not making wine, but
threshing wheat. Do you know how difficult it is to thresh grain
by letting the wind separate the chaff from the grain? Gideon
must be picking up the kernels of wheat, one grain at a time.
Gideon is understandably terrified by a divine encounter, yet the
angel of the Lord greets him as a warrior. His pedigree is mini-
mal, as Gideon himself recognizes; his clan is the weakest in the
tribe of Manasseh, and he is the runt of the family. Nevertheless,
God overlooks Gideon's fear and pedigree in recognition of
what he might become; they are not a factor in this story of call
and response.

There is good reason for Gideon's fear and reluctance to
lead. Marauding bands of Midianites have come up against the
land of Israel. Such annual attacks have been made possible by

the domestication of the camel. As a result, when local fields come to harvest, the Midianites can come quickly to take the produce of the land. Against this technological advantage, the Israelites are impoverished; they have little resources to resist the better-armed and mobile Midianite troops. The Israelites are forced to hide in the mountains, caves, and strongholds (6:2). They are in dismal straits!

There is an internal crisis as well. The Canaanite religion, with its promise of fertility for farmlands, lures Israel from obedience to God. Baal worship is established in Gideon's hometown—even in his own father's house—perhaps because of the apparent failure of their traditional faith.

Gideon is called out of an apostate household to initiate reform in his own village. After meeting the angel, he calls upon God to rescue him. The Lord says, "Peace be to you; do not fear, you shall not die" (6:23). He then builds an altar in his village in recognition that God is "peace," a symbol of a restored relationship (6:24).

This act is not enough. The altar to Baal on his father's property must be destroyed to complete the reform. Again showing his timidity, Gideon tears it down at night, replacing it with an altar to the Lord. The townspeople are furious and want to kill Gideon. However, Gideon's father comes to his defense and deflects the mob's anger with humor (6:31). Furthermore, it's his property, which explains why the townspeople back off from their vengeance.

Even in this moment, Gideon, now named Jerubbaal, which means "let Baal contend for himself," lacks courage and hides behind his father. He is not yet bold enough to come to his own defense (see 6:25-35). Even so, the internal threat has been met by the change in Gideon's home worship life. Gideon acts with subtlety; he begins his reform where it is most likely to succeed—at home with himself and his father. The external threat can now be addressed.

Thanks, but No Thanks
When troops are asked, "Who will volunteer for this mission?"

the expectation is that all of them will raise their hands. This is
what seems to have happened when Gideon assembled the men
of Israel. But surprisingly, rather than go into battle with this im-
pressive army, God tells Gideon to cull the troops by asking,
"Who is afraid and shaking in his sandals?" In response, 22,000
men are sent home, leaving 10,000 troops (7:3). Yet from God's
point of view, this is still too many!

God's next winnowing order baffles scholars. The volun-
teers act in two different ways in response to their thirst: one
group laps water like a dog; the other kneels and cups their
hands to bring water to their mouths. Gideon is to dismiss those
who cup their hands and keep those who lap. He is left with 300
fighting men. Many theories behind God's reasoning abound.
Some suggest that one method implies caution and the other ani-
mal instinct. Someone who tried lapping water concluded that
the mirror effect of water allows the lapper to survey what's
going on behind him- or herself. The other procedure is riskier,
since the drinker can only see what's in front. Whatever the reason, my answer has always been, and remains, that we simply
don't know and aren't expected to understand.

The biblical text explains the reason for the reduction: if
numbers were to determine the outcome, there would be no need
for God's direction and Israel would take the credit (7:2). It's not
simply that God doesn't need anyone. More to the point, God
needs people who are open to divine direction and alert enough
to avoid crumbling in a stressful situation. The selected people
have a capacity to live in a conflicted and threatening situation,
which is exactly what one wants in a battle situation.

Gideon's Call and Conviction

Like many of us, Gideon wrestles with his call and wants assurance that God will be with him. As a young boy, I can remember my parents talking about putting the fleece out to know
God's will. This was a direct reference to Judges 6:36-40.
Gideon receives an answer on two different occasions confirm-
ing that God will deliver Israel from the Midianites. In our lives,
we too look for assurance that the course we are taking follows
God's will.

After selecting the troops, God asks Gideon if he is still afraid. God knows Gideon, and God does not want a skittish commander. To allay this fear, God tells Gideon to go to the camp of the enemy. When Gideon and his servant arrive in the camp, they hear a Midianite recounting a dream about a barley cake tumbling into the camp and overturning it. So that there can be no mistake in Gideon's mind, his servant declares: "This is no other than the sword of Gideon . . . [and] into his hand God has given Midian and all the army" (7:14).

Gideon's first thought is not, "Wow, I'm going to win after all!" His first thought is to kneel down and pray. The Hebrew word *shchch*, translated "worship" in our text, implies a sense of reverence and humiliation before God. Gideon is grateful that God is directing his life. He knows that all things are in God's hands. The dream is not cause for arrogance, but for reverence and awe. From this point in the narrative, Gideon acts with certitude and serenity. The fears, so symptomatic of his earlier life, have disappeared; he has become a leader that no one but God could have anticipated.

There is no delay now. He tells his troops to get up and move quickly with a battle plan that will never appear in a war manual. Israel's weapons, if one can call them that, are impoverished and unexpected. Gideon's army uses trumpets, jars, and torches to create confusion. Victory comes, not through military might, but through fear and intimidation. In a wild battle, the Midianites self-destruct and flee for their lives (7:19-23). Israel is rid of the Midianite menace.

So What Did We Learn, Class?

There are tensions in this narrative. The two names for the lead character—Gideon and Jerubbaal—reflect the fact of two different worlds. The marauders are identified as Midianites and Amalekites, two very different nationalities. The narrative is hard to follow at times and appears to be made up of various snippets, like items in a newspaper gathered up over time. Much research has been directed to the sources that make up this larger narrative in Judges 6–8. It is important to remember that these stories circulated when there was centralized control in Israel. Different tribes told the stories in different ways, and their competing versions mattered. The snippets are collected in such a way that much of the independence of the sources is respected. Thus we have a narrative that preserves different textures and outlooks, all simultaneously visible in this one large collection of material.

The editor of this material sees repentance as the basis for renewal. Thus the first acts of Gideon are to reform his own household; such activity leads to a renewal of energy in the life of Israel. The final episode of the story seeks to entrench power in the hands of this newfound leader. The Israelites want to make Gideon into a king. He refuses in one of the most powerful denials found in scripture: "I will not rule over you, and my son will not rule over you; the LORD will rule over you" (8:23). Gideon has learned that God provides the victory, and upon this power the people are called to rely. There is no reason to change. First the Israelites copied their neighbors and worshiped their gods. Now even in victory they want to imitate their neighbors and be ruled by a king. Gideon tells them that it is possible to live without royalty.

It would be nice to tie up this story with, "And they lived happily ever after," but real life is more ambiguous. Though Gideon rejects a crown, he does fashion an ephod out of some of the gold taken in battle. An ephod is nothing more than a vest that holds the Urim and Thummim, which are used to determine the will of God (see Exodus 28 and 29). But does the making of an ephod constitute apostasy? Clearly this editor thought so, for "it became a snare to Gideon and to his family" (8:27*b*).

However, this comes on the heels of one of the most powerful declarations of the sovereignty of God in the Bible. My own view is that Gideon was providing a way for people to determine the will of God in the casting of these lots. Thus he remained true to his own vision.

If this was apostasy, it would be the first case in the book of Judges in which the revolt against God occurred in the lifetime of the one who delivered the Israelites. Verse 33 says that the relapse happened after Gideon's death. What is important for us is to reflect on the multivalent voices within the text that encourage us to appropriate these stories for our own generation.

Discussion and Action

1. Gideon claims an insignificant background that some might consider unimportant. Are there individuals in your community from particular regions, faith backgrounds, or cultural backgrounds who are automatically excluded from leadership? Have you been on the receiving end of such a snub?

2. Gideon's claim that his clan is the weakest in his tribe and that he is the least in his family speaks to his own sense of unimportance. How has your self-image, or a self-image imposed by others, shaped the way you respond to a call to the various ministries of the church? When have you said yes despite a poor self-image? What happened?'

3. The Midianites' pattern of economic oppression would seem to make the creation of good relationships impossible. Is it possible to reach out successfully to groups that we consider enemies? What about nations or cultures that want to reach out to us, but because of political, cultural, religious, or historical considerations it appears as if we have been the ones to blunt contact and relationship? How do we break down decades, or even centuries, of animosity?

4. The author makes a point of the Midianites' technological advantage. What effect has the apparent technological advantage of first world nations over developing nations had on competing economies? Reflect on the experiences of nations that have made the jump from third to first world technologies and economies.

5. Which false gods tempt us in times of national emergency, financial meltdown, and natural disaster? The angel proclaims peace to Gideon, but requires the destruction of the false gods to begin liberation. What barriers have you had to remove to open the doors to spiritual and emotional healing?

6. When, if ever, have you used your own version of Gideon's fleece to test a call to God's work? What were the results?

7. Despite victory, Gideon's choices are subject to more than one interpretation. Talk about times you or your church made strides, yet seemed to struggle with some of the same old problems. What lessons do you derive from Gideon's story? Which part of his life would you lift up? Which parts make you uncomfortable?

8. God seems to demonstrate infinite patience with Gideon's uncertainty. What does this say about God? About Gideon? How much patience do you require of others, and are you able to be patient with them?

6

Jotham's Fable and Abimelech's Design for Kingship
Judges 9

Personal Preparation

1. Read Judges 9 in its entirety. Draw a flowchart that shows the relationships of the characters and how they change over the course of the chapter.
2. Learn "There is a balm in Gilead," and bring a copy of the song to the session.
3. Write a sentence or two about "repentance" and "compassion," two key themes in this text, and bring your descriptions of these terms to the session.
4. Research a tribal rivalry that troubles the world, especially if it troubles your region. Discover, if you can, the roots of the rivalry, and the consequences—both in the past and the present.
5. Recall a favorite fable from your youth to share with the rest of the group.

Suggestions for Sharing and Prayer

1. Open with the Prayer of St. Francis (see the "Resource Pages" at the back of the book).
2. Sing "There is a balm in Gilead" as you gather together. Open with an invitation to prayer. Following this, take time for personal sharing. Offer a prayer of gratitude, intercession, discernment, etc., in response to each person's sharing.

3. Invite a couple of people to tell the fables they recalled from childhood. Have each storyteller comment on what this fable meant when they first heard it, and what it means to them now. How important is applicability in these stories?
4. Discuss the roots of the tribal rivalries you researched. What are the competing viewpoints? Have there been peaceful resolutions to some problems? Has there been violence? What would you say to individuals involved in these conflicts if you could speak to them? What would they say to you? Tie the Prayer of St. Francis to these questions. What answers might this prayer provide?
5. Sing "There is a balm in Gilead" again. Close by repeating the Prayer of St. Francis.

Understanding

In much of the Middle East, and in places like Afghanistan and Pakistan, identity is centered in one's tribe. These tribes are sometimes set against each another, and occasionally wreak havoc on one another.

This contemporary behavior should help us understand Abimelech's strategy. He manipulates the various tribes using relationships on his maternal side to stir up distrust of his brothers, who come from other tribal roots by virtue of marriage. Abimelech "said to . . . the whole clan of his mother's family . . . 'Which is better for you, that all seventy of the sons of Jerubbaal rule over you, or that one rule over you?' Remember also that I am your bone and your flesh" (9:1-2). Abimelech plays on the heartstrings of his relatives and clan association to rally their support. Notice in verse 3 that this alliance is based on kinship with the Shechemites as well, who are inclined to follow him on the basis of this affirmation: "He is our brother."

He also presents a major distortion, a straw dog if you will, that will become even more apparent in Jotham's fable. Abimelech fans the flames of fear through the specter of multi-headed rule, even though no one else has suggested that such a thing might happen. In fact, in our last study, Gideon made it clear that neither he nor his sons will rule over anyone. But Abimelech has decided that if he wants to be king, he must first forge an alliance based on the fear of outside intervention on the part of his brothers. When his fabricated fear campaign succeeds, he immediately "taxes" the population into giving him seventy pieces of silver, a hefty sum with which he can hire henchmen for his own private army.

Who are these followers? The text says that they are "worthless and reckless fellows" (v. 4). The first adjective is used much the same way in Proverbs 12:11 and 28:19, which essentially say that "those who till the land will have plenty of fruit, but those who follow worthlessness (*reqim*) lack heart or live in poverty." In other words, Abimelech's henchmen are people who are not gainfully employed and are not seeking work. The second word, "reckless," implies insolence and looseness. These people are troublemakers. They are not workers, but idlers who stand on the sidelines waiting for mischief.

With a band of ruffians in place, Abimelech is now ready to do his dirty work. He returns to his father's house and kills all his brothers, with the exception of Jotham, who hides himself. Such tribal violence seems commonplace, not only in a book like Judges, but in traditional societies even today where long-term grudges, disputes over lands and inheritance, and distinct genealogies separate neighbors and make them enemies. Think about the Serbs and Albanians, Hutus and Tutsis, Pashtuns and Hazaras, even Catholics and Protestants in Ireland. In tribal structures, real or imagined wrongs centuries-old are more real than any actual contemporary events. For this reason, cohesive alliances are impossible unless an outside force threatens their existence.

Having cleared the decks of any rivals, Abimelech returns to Shechem and is made king—a direct violation of the desire and commitment of his father, Gideon. The people share the blame, for they have given up their freedoms without ever seriously considering whether they need a king!

Tell Me a Story

Jotham—his family's lone survivor—comes out of hiding to tell the lords of Shechem a fable. A fable is a story that generally uses animals, but in some cases vegetation, to make a point. In this account, the point is clear. The trees have gathered to select a king; in turn they ask the olive tree, the fig tree, and the vine to rule over them. Each declines on the basis that they have too much to do. The olive tree produces oil by which gods and mortals are honored. The fig tree produces a sweet and delicious fruit for all to enjoy. The vine produces wine that cheers both gods and mortals. Why would any one of them give up their productive life to rule over the other vegetation? Their answer is consistent: they are engaged and have no time to be king.

Who then can be king? Only one who has nothing else to do. In this fable, the bramble offers shade—which as we know will squeeze the life out of the other trees. As the bramble grows and covers the vegetation beneath it, it destroys all life. This dim view of royalty will be more clearly articulated later by the prophet Samuel. A king, Samuel tells Israel, "will take your daughters to be perfumers and cooks and bakers. He will take the best of your fields and vineyards and olive orchards and give them to his courtiers. He will take one-tenth of your grain and of your vineyards . . . . He will take your male and female slaves, and the best of your cattle and donkeys, and put them to his work. He will take one-tenth of your flocks, and you shall be his slaves" (1 Samuel 8:13-17). In other words, God's people will lose all they have to feed the king's appetite. This revenue will buy implements of war and equipment for his chariots (1 Samuel 8:12). A king will seek to protect his own authority through the accumulation of power at the expense of the governed. The meaning of the fable seems clear: Abimelech's rule will squeeze the productive lives of the people.

The fable also reflects Abimelech's choice of followers. They are the ones in the society who have nothing better to do. The language of worthless and loose fellows parallels a group in Proverbs who do not toil or work for their survival (cf. 28:19).

They create mischief and violence and make no significant contribution to the life of Shechem. Abimelech's reign, in the end, will be nothing more than a brief interval brought by a petty chieftain who has little on his side but a relentless drive to power. He is a perfect example of the adage, the higher the monkey climbs the more you see of his behind.

Come and Go
The narrative of Abimelech reflects a fractured society whose turmoil is fed by distrust. It shouldn't be surprising that the people of Shechem come under the influence of another faction—that of Gaal, son of Ebed, who ridicules Abimelech and his heritage. Implicit in the text is the need for even larger troops to sustain power against the rising tide of dissent (v. 29). We find two parties vying for power, and the old tribal allegiances come back into play. The conflict continues over time, with different parties ascending and descending. It's hard to know who remains in power.

In the end, Abimelech meets his death at the hand of a woman who throws a millstone on his head. In his dying agony, he asks his armor bearer to kill him because he does not want to be remembered as the great warrior killed by a woman. Despite this, scripture will later ask: "Who killed Abimelech son of Jerubbaal? Did not a woman throw an upper millstone on him from the wall, so that he died at Thebez?" (2 Samuel 11:21).

Once again, in the book of Judges we see that God does not require an army or high-tech weapons for the divine will to be done. And, once again, God stands against an oppressor and with the oppressed.

The greatest irony in the story is that the name, Abimelech, means "God is my father." He is named for the basic belief of his father, Gideon, that God—not one of his sons—would rule over Israel. The narrative ends by simply saying that all the Israelites went home, and God repaid Abimelech for the crime he committed against his father in killing his seventy brothers.

Discussion and Action

1. Share more of the fables people recalled from their youth. Why are these fables memorable? Find out if everyone in the group finds the same meaning in each fable, or if more than one meaning might be apparent. How can such stories bring clarity to situations that mere explanation fails to do?

2. After playing upon the fears of the tribes, Abimelech is installed as king. After the events of September 11, 2001, many people felt fear and reacted in alarm. Lawmakers and citizens seemed willing to give up basic rights because of that fear. What is your memory of the alarm you or others felt? What was your feeling at the time about measures that were taken? How do you feel about these measures now?

3. Have you ever watched anyone use fear to manipulate people? Describe what happened. What fears cause you to think or act irrationally?

4. Share what group members learned about the sources of tribal rivalries (see "Personal Preparation"). To what extent do you sympathize with these feelings? Are there ways in which they seem incomprehensible? What attitudes, prejudices, or preferences do you have that might seem puzzling to others?

5. Discuss your sentences about "compassion" and "repentance." Share stories of how you have put these into practice in your own lives.

6. After the death of Osama bin Laden, the Dalai Lama, a well-known pacifist, said that although he would avoid killing mosquitoes unless there was a danger of malaria, sometimes people reap the consequences of what they have sown. Discuss the end of dictators and other cruel individuals that you have heard of in your lifetime. Was justice done in these instances? Do the actions of despots that cost many lives justify using violence against them? What are some alternative solutions, and how might they be enacted?

7

Ammonite Aggression and the Desire for More Land

Judges 10–11

Personal Preparation

1. Read Judges 10 and 11. Take note of the list of minor judges in 10:1-5. What is similar and what is different in the cyclical repetition of Israel's dysfunction?
2. Study a Bible map from this period. Locate Ammon and the other nations of the Transjordan as background to this session.
3. Revisit the sentences you wrote for session 6 on "repentance" and "compassion." These are two key components in this session's text as well. Bring your revised descriptions of these terms to the session.
4. Research and prepare music or a digital download of "Deep river" for the session.

Suggestions for Sharing and Prayer

1. There is a deep sadness undergirding this story, even though it ends with a military triumph. "Deep river" also has an underlying sadness, even though it speaks hopefully of crossing over the Jordan. As a group, sing it slowly and sadly as you begin your time together.
2. To the extent that you feel safe, relate incidents in your lives that ended with unintended consequences. Talk about what original intentions there may have been, but

how circumstances went spiraling into a different direction. If you have no personal incidents you wish to share, reflect on church, historical, or national circumstances.

3. Jephthah and the king of the Ammonites discover they have a different version of historical events. Is there a story from your church's history, family history, or local history in which there are conflicting viewpoints? Describe these conflicts and discuss the validity of the differing viewpoints.

4. In Jephthah's culture, an oath was binding, even if the consequences, as in this case, are disastrous. Role-play a scenario in which Jephthah meets with your group to discuss the situation regarding his vow and what is required of him. What emotions does your discussion elicit? What options, if any, come to the fore? How does the role-playing end?

5. Select one section (or one verse) of the story of Jephthah and read it out loud. Invite each person to choose one word that stands out to them. Prayerfully lift up these words in silence, allowing your minds—and the Spirit— to shape your thoughts. Listen. After a minute, read the selection aloud again. With another person in the group, reflect on what that word says about your shared ministries and relationships. After another minute, reread the selection aloud a third time. Together, pray about the way words can speak to us, thanking the Spirit for new insights.

6. Close with prayer for yourselves and for all who face difficult circumstances. Sing "Deep river" once more.

Understanding

Border disputes often erupt between neighboring states. One example is the disputed border between Belize and Guatemala in Central America. Some Guatemalan maps depict Belize as a Guatemalan province, for which there is no historical precedent. As we shall see in this session, the king of Ammon's border dispute also includes a claim for which there is no historical precedent.

Ammon's incursions against Israel are to reclaim land occupied by Israel after the defeat of Sihon three hundred years earlier. The Ammonites want to move into territory populated by the central tribes, particularly Ephraim, Judah, and Benjamin, along with the Gileadites, who are in Transjordan.

The dispute is about borders, much like the conflict with the Philistines in the story of Samson that follows this one. Israel is hemmed in on both sides by strong enemies who have military might, including weapons of iron, which Israel did not have (see 1 Samuel 13:22). It was an act of aggression when the Ammonites crossed over the Jordan.

The problem was more than just a matter of borders. Israel had adopted the religion of Canaan. Israel had forsaken the God who delivered them out of slavery, and instead worshiped the pantheon of Canaanite fertility gods to assure crop success. Their lack of faithfulness left the Israelites defenseless.

This seesaw pattern of belief and disbelief is woven throughout the book of Judges. Again and again, Israel loses its divine protection when the people are unfaithful. After they repent and cry out for deliverance, a strong charismatic leader appears on the scene and delivers them from oppression. Israel then forgets its origins and backslides once more into idolatry, falls into distress, and seeks deliverance. This pattern repeats itself throughout the book. In this chapter, the community is again lost and in distress. What is it to do?

Repentance and God's Response

Those who struggle with addictive behaviors sometimes have to hit rock bottom before they are ready to change. The first step back is to seek help. After many years of oppression and distress, this is what Israel does. They finally cry out to God. The Hebrew verb *za'aq* (cry out) denotes a shout of desperation, despair, and bitterness. This happens when an individual or community doesn't know what to do and has run out of solutions. Backs against the wall, there is no escape. This moment prompts a redirection in life because that is all that is left to do, much as the prodigal in Jesus' parable in Luke 15. This shout is the primal scream for help and assistance.

The second step is to make a confession: "We have sinned against you, because we have abandoned our God and have worshiped the Baals" (Judges 10:10). The word for sin used here implies missing the mark, going astray, heading in the wrong direction. The people admit they have moved away from God and abandoned their past relationship. This implies divorce—a radical separation that really asks whether return is possible. Yet the people seem sincere in their desire to change direction.

God replies that they should go and cry to the gods whom they have been serving and let them deliver them from distress. This answer seems like a taunt. How do we account for God's response? The bottom line is that God's doubt about their confession brings a more serious redirection. Look what is reported next. The third step in the response is action: "So they put away the foreign gods from among them" (v. 16). The Hebrew word for "repentance," even though it doesn't appear here, is *shub*, which is an action verb meaning "to turn around." Without action, words are meaningless. In the end Israel puts itself completely in the hands of God: "Do to us whatever seems good" (v. 15).

At the conclusion of this account, the text states that the Lord "could no longer bear to see Israel suffer" (v. 16). Some don't expect to find this level of God's love in the Hebrew Bible. Yet, it is where the story of Israel began: "I have observed the misery of my people who are in Egypt; I have heard their cry on account of their taskmasters. Indeed, I know their sufferings, and I have come down to deliver them from the Egyptians" (Exodus 3:7-8*a*). A similar disposition is displayed by God centuries later in Hosea 11: "When Israel was a child, I loved him . . . . I led them with cords of human kindness, with bands of love . . . . How can I give you up, Ephraim? How can I hand you over, O Israel? . . . My heart recoils within me; my compassion grows warm and tender. I will not execute my fierce anger . . . for I am God and no mortal" (vv. 1, 4, 8-9). These passages from all periods of Israel's life point to the compassionate nature of God.

Divine Reconciliation Leads to Human Reconciliation

With a new perspective on life, the Gileadites summon Jephthah to lead them into battle. This is a bit strange, since, as the son of a prostitute, Jephthah had been kicked out of his father's home. His brothers wanted nothing to do with him and did not want him to share in the inheritance. Now, they are forced to come to him for help. He is not a paragon of virtue, since he has collected a band of renegades to make raids. Nonetheless, his prowess makes him the most likely candidate to lead Gilead in battle against the Ammonites.

He agrees to do this upon one condition—they have to bring him home again (Judges 11:9). The word translated as "bring home" comes from the same Hebrew word that is used for "repentance." This is a remarkable turn of events, since his brothers have to swallow their pride and make him leader over their troops. I find it a striking parallel to the events in the preceding passage. A wrong has been righted and restoration has occurred. However, the story of reconciliation does not stop here. Jephthah does not leap into battle, but rather sues for peace. He seeks a nonviolent resolution first.

After being named head of the troops, Jephthah sends messengers to the king of the Ammonites to find out what this fight is about (v. 12). Such behavior is informed by the drift of a story of reconciliation. Jephthah would like to avoid battle, and so acts diplomatically.

The king of Ammon replies with a lie—accusing Israel of taking his land. Actually Ammon did not own the land at that time, as Jephthah makes clear in his reply. Rather than calling the king a liar, which would leave no room for negotiation, he lays out Israel's claim. When Israel first came in contact with the countries of the Transjordan, they came in peace. Israel asked permission to pass through the lands of Edom and Moab, but was refused. As a result, they did not enter those lands. In other words, Israel respected the territorial rights of these two countries.

When Israel instead asked to go through land on the other side of the Arnon River, a free territory that was not owned by

Moab but was under the reign of an Amorite king, the king in this area, Sihon, immediately set out to destroy Israel and was defeated. Thus the land fell into Israelite hands some three hundred years earlier. The king of Ammon was trying to lay claim to land that had never belonged to his people, to which Jephthah asks whether Ammon wants to suffer the same consequences (v. 23). We know through archeology that Ammon did not move this far west until the twelfth century BCE.

Jephthah cites a story about King Balak, who tried to get rid of Israel by having it cursed by a prophet (see Numbers 22–24). This effort failed. There is recognition of divinely appointed land for both Ammon and Moab, but it does not include Heshbon and its villages and Aroer and its villages, which had been occupied by Israel for three hundred years. Why change landscape after all this time? Jephthah does not act out of spite or hatred, but tries to reason diplomatically by citing historical precedent, which is a rather interesting approach given these chaotic stories. As Sarah Niditch explains in *War in the Hebrew Bible*, such reasoning assumes a just war theory, for "to fight without just cause is to do evil. The group whose cause is just will prevail" (126).

The Failure of Diplomacy and Jephthah's Fatal Flaw
Ultimately diplomacy fails. Jephthah tried to live within the context of reconciliation with God. But he makes a tragic mistake when he tries to control God by making an oath to sacrifice the first creature that greets him on his return home if he is victorious in battle. As it turns out, his daughter greets him, rather than one of the animals.

Despite the fact that such a practice violates the fundamental nature of Israelite belief and breaks the ban on the sacrifice of children or adults that runs throughout Israel's legal and narrative texts, daughter and father go through with her death. Just when wisdom is embraced in a profound way through diplomatic pursuits, it is disrupted by the desire to secure success by any means. Isn't this like most of us, who seek to secure God's favor by promising this or that, thereby failing to live by the gift of

God's grace? The outcome of such reasoning leads to disaster, and one of the most troubling outcomes in the book of Judges.

Discussion and Action

1. In looking at past conflicts where the combatants had different views of history, which is easier to adopt—the viewpoint of the side that won or of the side that lost? Think of historical situations in which you share the viewpoint of the winning side, and those where you share the perspective of the losing side.

2. Jephthah seems to be alienated from his father, at least from his father's family. How did this color his attitude when it came to helping his people?

3. The story concludes with Jephthah's rash vow that results in the sacrifice of his daughter. Though such vows were to be taken very seriously, do you think it would have been better for him to break this vow? Why, or why not? How often have you heard someone say, "Swear to God," without considering the consequences?

4. In some ways Judges is a love story between God and the people. How many times should God forgive? How many times are you able to forgive? Should there be limits to forgiveness between people, or between God and the people? Why, or why not?

5. Together, Tola and Jair judge over Israel for forty-five years (see Judges 10:1-5). This nearly half-century of peace produces little notice for these two. Why is it that sometimes those who do well are overlooked, while difficult behavior often attracts attention? Who are some "unsung heroes" deserving of greater recognition?

6. Read aloud and compare the definitions of "repentance" and "compassion" that you wrote prior to the session. What similarities and differences do you note? How have you experienced these things in your life? What, if anything, changed in your thinking between the last session and this one?

7. Jephthah was rejected by his people and considered an outcast until they were desperate, after which they called upon him to be their deliverer. Should he have been grateful? How might you have responded in that situation? When have you observed rejection followed by acceptance?

8

Obedience and the Story of Samson
Judges 13–16

Personal Preparation

1. Take time to reflect on what you know about Samson before you read Judges 13–16 and this session. If it helps you to remember, jot down your impressions. After reading, look back at your list. How do these four chapters confirm or change your previous impressions of this judge?

2. Review the laws regarding the nazirite vow in Numbers 6:1-21. Do some research in a Bible dictionary, commentary, or on the Internet for more information about what it means to be a nazarite. Take your notes along to the session.

3. Prepare to sing or listen to "Steal away" during the session.

Suggestions for Sharing and Prayer

1. Greet one another with news of the week. Sing "Steal away." Invite prayers led by individuals in the group.

2. Review what you have learned about the various judges—not only what they accomplished, but how they did it. How do they measure up to your idea of leadership? What does this say about your potential for leadership? What does this suggest about what God might consider to be qualifications for leadership?

3. How would Samson's life be viewed and reported through the lens of our 24-7 news outlets? Would this be a good thing or a bad thing for Samson's development as an adult?
4. What role did Samson's parents play in the development of their son's values? What role did your parents or mentors play in the establishment of yours?
5. Discuss situations in which grown children have ended up with very different values from their parents—for good or ill. What does this reality suggest about the extent to which parents are responsible for their children's choices, especially after they are grown? In the situations you are thinking about, to what extent do you think parents contributed to changes for the worse or to changes for the better? What part does free will play in the choices the next generation makes?
6. Invite individual prayers for the family situations brought up in your sharing time. Also, pray for one another and for the choices each generation must make. Close by singing "Steal away" once more.

Understanding

The last chapter in my doctoral dissertation, *The Annunciation in Old Testament Birth Stories*, was on Judges 13, the birth narrative of Samson. Nowhere in scripture does the devotion of a mother stand out more than here. It was a reminder of my own mother's desire for me and my sister to live a devout life. As she explained to us many times, not a day went by that she didn't pray for us. Among the many memories of my mother, her daily kneeling in prayer is a constant reminder of her care for me.

When I visited this chapter after forty-two years, I found myself reflecting on Samson's mother and her life in the world of the judges. Most stories in Judges are about violence and warfare, deceit and oppression, and intertribal squabbles. The opening verse notes that society itself was in chaos, unsure about what values are important, and how to adjust to a settled state after a nomadic existence. In contrast, the rest of this chapter and the book of Ruth, with which we will end this study, are devoted to family values, and suggest that family plays a powerful role in the formation of individuals. The pattern of obedience in the life of Samson is set within the framework of his family and the devotion of his mother.

The Regimen of Obedience

Even before his birth, Samson's mother, who is never named, is to follow the first vow of a nazirite: "They shall separate themselves from wine and strong drink; they shall drink no wine vinegar or other vinegar, and shall not drink any grape juice or eat grapes, fresh or dried. All their days as nazirites they shall eat nothing that is produced by the grapevine, not even the seeds or the skins" (Numbers 6:3-4). That she would accept such a requirement indicates that Samson's family has not embraced Canaanite religion. They are obedient in an otherwise disobedient landscape. Samson's mother represents steadfastness to a regimen that her son was unlikely to adopt.

The second requirement of the nazirite vow falls upon the son: "No razor is to come on his head, for the boy shall be a nazirite to God from birth" (Judges 13:5). Hair is an outward symbol by which the nazarite was known as someone devoted solely to the Lord. Clearly, hair is the key motif of the story; hair is the source of Samson's strength and basic to the narrative. In ancient storytelling and through the ages, hair has been a symbol of a person's vitality. According to folk belief, possessing even a strand of hair of an enemy allowed a person to control or torture that individual (Soggin 258). The story line in Judges holds up the theme of obedience, which Samson's family typifies to a greater extent than the hero himself.

These chapters from Judges do not speak to all dimensions of the nazirite vow. There is no specific reference to the avoidance of corpses, although the reference to something unclean may imply that. Also, the vow was usually taken willingly, not imposed on an infant at birth, and usually did not last a lifetime. However, here the nazarite law is clearly tied to Samson's birth narrative in order to give the entire story a religious frame.

Again, the action of a woman stands out. She seems to know more about God than her husband does. In the exchange after the sacrifice and the disappearance of the angel, Manoah shakes in fear and says, "We shall surely die, for we have seen God" (13:22). But his wife calmly answers, "If the LORD had meant to kill us, he would not have accepted a burnt offering and a grain offering at our hands, or shown us all these things, or now announced to us such things as these" (13:23). This unnamed wife takes her place beside Rahab, Deborah, Jael, Ruth, and Naomi as heroines of the faith. In times of turmoil, women provide the ballast for men who live in fear.

In my estimation, the reason for including Samson's story is not only the theme of obedience, but also to illustrate the importance of family life in the context of displacement and oppression. This was the crisis facing those who were exiled in Babylon as they produced the final edition of this book. We know from sociological studies that the family is key to sustaining life and meaning among refugees. Family life is one of the alternative story lines for this period.

The Life and Death of Samson

Despite being brought up in his mother's obedient faith, Samson's life quickly unravels, as told in the stories that follow: a failed marriage, the allure of a prostitute, and—despite great physical exploits against the Philistines—seduction into revealing the secret of his power.

On the positive side of the ledger, he does remain faithful to his own kindred. When he hides out among the Judeans and the Philistines come to take him, he asks the Judeans not to harm him but to hand him over to the Philistines. The result is that the Judeans are spared and the Philistines defeated by the hand of Samson (15:9*ff*.). This is one of the few redeeming encounters in his life.

In the final scenes, we find him shorn of his power and degraded in prison. Samson had never led an army and always acted alone. He remained an isolated and tragic figure. Soggin observes that you either take Samson as a religious hero with tragic elements or as a nonhero whose example is to be avoided (258). I am inclined to view him as an individual who fulfilled his destiny in spite of himself. He does not elect obedience as a pattern for his life, but is forced into it by circumstance of birth and the circumstances of his imprisonment.

Ironically, once Samson is under lock and key, the limitations imposed in the Philistine prison require him to resume his nazarite regimen. The Philistines foolishly allow his hair to grow. I can hardly believe that he would be treated to wine or strong drink in prison. He was isolated and forced into obedience by the reality of his life in prison. One of the purposes of these narratives is to mock these dreaded conquerors who occupied the plains west of Israel, making them look weak-minded and arrogant as they make sport of a blind man. In deprivation, Samson becomes strong. The theme that is so fundamental to these narratives is reiterated here. In his imprisonment, Samson found the purpose that was entrusted to his mother at her first encounter with the angel: "It is he who shall begin to deliver Israel from the hand of the Philistines" (13:5*b*).

In the end, Samson fulfills his destiny and embraces his first loyalty with the words: "Lord GOD, remember me and strengthen me only this once, O God, so that with this one act of revenge I may pay back the Philistines for my two eyes" (16:28). His strength returns, and with it, he rededicates his life to the purpose for which he was created. He causes the collapse of a temple dedicated to a foreign god, much as Gideon destroyed the altar dedicated to Baal.

Yet even in this event that cost Samson his life, his obedience is more by default than design. In his apparent weakness he is restored to his birth-given purpose. This is a consistent theme in Judges: a man with a deformed hand, a bedouin woman without standing, a terrified farmer, and a banished son are now joined by a blind man in the continuing story of the defeat of Israel's enemies.

The story ends as it began—with Samson's family: "Then his brothers and all his family came down and took him and brought him up and buried him between Zorah and Eshtaol in the tomb of his father Manoah. He had judged Israel twenty years" (16:31). However, even with this, the destiny of his tribe, the Danites, was not fixed. They too would move to the north, undoubtedly because of a continued threat from the Philistines. The situation remains fluid and serves as a reminder to Israel in the exile that they are not the first to suffer displacement.

Discussion and Action

1. Samson's mother seems to have had a very practical opinion about God. As she pointed out to her husband, if God had wanted to kill them, their offering would not have been accepted. She was also devoted to her faith, not only in word but in practice. Talk about the people who set a faith example for you—parents, mentors, pastors, teachers, etc.

2. The author talks about the importance of family in creating identity, whether in a time of cultural and political dissolution such as the setting of Judges, or in the context of exile when the book was written. How has your family, whether biological or spiritual, had a hand in your formation? In what crucibles has your faith been tested?

3. What was your opinion of Samson before reading this session? How did it change afterward? In what ways does his failure to learn embody the cyclical dysfunction of Israel? To what extent does the health or dysfunction of society impact the life of an individual, and how do you think the lives of individuals change their societies?

4. Depending on how you view Samson, his life can be seen as one of great achievement or one of great failure. Discuss leaders who have been both admirable and flawed. What do you suppose Samson could have accomplished if he had been able to overcome some of his flaws?

5. The author makes the point that taking nazirite vows is usually an adult decision, whereas in the case of Samson the choice was made for him by his parents. In your

opinion, was that an appropriate action? What does this suggest when it comes to the differences between infant and adult baptism?

6. Samson's religious vows set him apart—not only from other nations, but also from his own people. When do you notice the different religious practices of others, both in and outside of Christianity? How tolerant of others are you? How tolerant do you find your local community? Have you experienced more tolerance or intolerance in your religious practice?

9

The Consequences of Violence
Judges 19–21

Personal Preparation

1. Make a list of the biblical judges you recall. Write a sentence about each judge, describing what they accomplished and how they accomplished it.
2. Read Judges 19–21. Write down your thoughts about how this section differs from the other portions of Judges that you have studied.
3. Obtain the music or a digital download of "Ezekiel saw the wheel." Bring the lyrics to the session. Also, take time to read the poem, "The Second Coming," by W. B. Yeats, printed in the resources at the end of this book.

Suggestions for Sharing and Prayer

1. Greet each other with the sign of peace. (One says, "The peace of the blessed Lord be yours," and another responds with, "We share this selfsame peace.") Share events from the past week. Sing "Ezekiel saw the wheel" together. The leader may lead in prayer.
2. Make quick plans for next week's wrap-up session, including assignments for bringing refreshments.
3. Share your lists of judges (see "Personal Preparation"). How many judges in total did the group recall? Which judges does the group consider to have accomplished the most? Which ones accomplished the least?

4. Turn to the poem, "The Second Coming" by W. B. Yeats, printed in the resources at the end of this book. The poem combines Christian and non-Christian images in a foreboding jumble. It was written in 1919 following the chaos of World War I. Read the poem aloud. Compare some of the strange images to the chaos described in Judges 19–21. How do you react to the poem? How do you react to this section of Judges? What does it mean to say that the center cannot hold, that things fall apart, and that anarchy is loosed upon the world? Where do you see that in Judges? Where have you seen that in your own lifetime? What part has your faith played in addressing the horrors that have occurred in modern times?

5. As a group, brainstorm about how the violence of these chapters could have been forestalled. Would mediation have been possible? In current situations, as well as in the time of the judges, how can communication or reconciliation take place when the world seems to be falling apart?

6. Close with prayer for the world's suffering.

Understanding

As we have already observed in the narratives of Gideon and Abimelech, the compiler of Judges harbors suspicion about kingly rule. Throughout the book there are episodes describing the overthrow of local kings who oppress the people. The implication is that when it comes to deliverance, God will assist and leadership will be inspired. Once the challenge has been met, true leadership should avoid entrenching itself in power.

In the debate about the selection of a king, there is a definite antimonarchical cast to the speeches of Samuel (1 Samuel 8, 12). The prophet insists that choosing a king goes counter to the will of God. The book of Ruth, which concludes our study, emphasizes that a just society can arise out of the diligent action of citizens who work to protect the unprotected. In fact, even a foreigner can fulfill the full range of the law. No king is needed in a just society. This outlook is accentuated by the opening of the book: "In the days when the judges ruled" (Ruth 1:1).

Judges 19–21 portrays a different analysis of this same time period. This narrative describes an escalation of violence in a power vacuum. I believe the author's purpose is clearly stated in the opening and concluding lines of this narrative complex: "In those days, when there was no king in Israel" (19:1*a*) and "In those days there was no king in Israel; all the people did what was right in their own eyes" (21:25). The problem, according to the editor of this material, is a lack of centralized authority. The situation calls for a different system of governance. The answer is a king. This narrative complex then serves as the introduction to the search for a king in 1 Samuel.

This development seems a bit strange, given the long years of struggle against this type of authority, but perhaps it lies in the nature of the human condition. After they dethroned King Louis XVI, the French people reverted to extreme violence that ended in the Reign of Terror. Executions were a daily occurrence as the ruling party attempted to rid France of any unrepublican proponents. In the end, a new centralized authority emerged under Napoleon, not unlike the sweep of history under review in Judges and Samuel.

Things Fall Apart

The story begins quietly enough with a Levite seeking the return of his estranged wife in the town of Bethlehem. He goes to the home of his father-in-law and speaks tenderly with his concubine. He takes additional donkeys so that apparently she can ride back home with him. His intent is to bring her home, and he succeeds in consoling her. Hospitality is provided by the father-in-law and the marriage appears to be restored. After days of feasting, the Levite, his concubine, and his servant head home. Because of a late start, they need to stop for the night. But where?

The Levite decides not to stay among foreigners in Jebus (Jerusalem), but among kinfolk in the Benjaminite town of Gibeah, where he could rightly expect that hospitality would be extended to a relative. However, no one from the town offers a safe haven, until a fellow Ephraimite—both he and the Levite were from the hill country of Ephraim—extends hospitality. This is not what we expect. The "all Israel" of the Joshua narratives has fractured, and one tribe is foreign to another.

In a scene reminiscent of Sodom and Gomorrah, those expected to offer hospitality seek to violate the Levite. In desperation he throws out his concubine, who is abused all night and dies. The next morning he orders her to get up and get going. When he realizes she is dead, he puts her on a donkey and leaves. Once home, he hews her into twelve pieces and sends them to the twelve tribes of Israel with a message: "Thus shall you say to all the Israelites, 'Has such a thing ever happened since the day that the Israelites came up from the land of Egypt until this day? Consider it, take counsel, and speak out'" (19:30). Violence happens at two levels—the rape and murder of the concubine, and the desecration of her corpse: desecration in life and also in death.

Violence against the living and the dead. Whatever social compact might have been in place is dissolving.

The Center Cannot Hold

The violence escalates. The other tribes ask the Benjaminites to turn over the individuals who perpetrated this crime. Benjamin refuses, probably on the grounds that the perpetrators were close relatives—and tribal obligations trumped requirements of justice. As a result, war breaks out, and all but six hundred males from the tribe of Benjamin are killed (20:47). The Israelites now have concern and compassion for Benjamin, and seek to find wives for these remaining men. This proves difficult, since all the other tribes took an oath not to provide wives for anyone from Benjamin.

A remedy is found, but it comes as a result of further violence. Because no one from Jabesh-gilead answered the call to assemble with all the other tribes, they are obliterated—with the exception of four hundred virgins (21:12). But that does not provide enough wives, so additional women are kidnapped.

The whole narrative is appalling. Violence begets further atrocities. Why is this narrative in the Bible? Clearly there is a collapse of the moral compass, such as what we find in the violence perpetrated by Tutsis on Hutus, Hindus on Muslims, German gentiles on German Jews, Serbs on Albanians. When violence erupts, neighbors go after one another with murderous intent.

More Anarchy Loosed upon the World

In his work, *Identity and Violence*, Amartya Sen observes: "The martial art of fostering violence draws on basic instincts and uses them to crowd out the freedom to think and the possibility of composed reasoning. But it also draws on a kind of logic—a fragmentary logic. The specific identity that is separated out for special action is, in most cases, a genuine identity . . . a Hutu is indeed a Hutu . . . a Serb is not an Albanian. What is done to turn the sense of self-understanding into a murderous instrument is (1) to ignore the relevance of other affiliations and associations, and (2) to redefine the demands of the 'sole' identity in a particular belligerent form" (275*ff.*). In the end, whole classes of people suffer violent action, as portrayed in this narrative from Judges. As we have already noted, there is hardly a moment of composed logic in any part of this story.

No one in this story is named—unlike the narrative that follows in the book of Ruth, where all the key figures are named. Part of the logic of genocide is to ignore or remove personal identity. In this narrative, tribal identities are pitted against one another. Solutions to knotty problems are met with violence that has a cascading effect. Violence leads to more violence, including the desecration of the dead. Tribes are united by vengeance without considering the consequences. Exasperated, the editor of this work speaks for the rest of us: "All the people did what was right in their own eyes" (21:25). For the compiler of the tradition, this narrative cements the case for a king.

Darkness Drops Again

So, what about us? In the narrative, the reduction of people to simple labels—Benjaminite, Levite, Ephraimite, concubine, old man—leads to violence. In the contemporary setting, we may say: "She's a Muslim. He's gay. He's a liberal." We could expand the list indefinitely. Amartya Sen shows how the reduction of identity to one word destroys the individuality of each person: "I am an American. I worship in a Protestant congregation. I love gardening. I study and write about the Old Testament. I am a husband and father." However, when we expand our understanding of a specific individual into a multifold identity that encompasses all these elements, we will be less prone to do violence. At one level, the narrative illustrates this point, and may serve as an illustration of how narrowing identity leads to violence.

Discussion and Action

1. How is your opinion about the book of Judges changed by this study? Is it inevitable that a society will experience some level of breakdown? Sometimes violence breaks out because there is a shortage of food, resources, land, opportunity, or vision. Sometimes there is misinformation (or perhaps accurate information) perpetrated about other groups that incites people to horrifying action. What do you think are the causes of this breakdown?

2. According to the mathematics of the Cascade Theory, individuals are much more likely to reach the wrong conclusion or make bad choices if they are near people who have made a wrong conclusion or bad choice. These things cascade, and people begin to espouse opinions or take actions they would not have in other circumstances. Have you ever been caught up in the emotion of others? What were your thoughts at the time? Afterward, how did you feel about your emotions, what you said, or the actions you took?

3. If you could speak to the characters in this story, what would you say? Is it possible to speak or witness when violence is rampant? Is it possible to anticipate the escalation of violence? Speak together about instances where genocide, violence, and chaos have emerged in history and in your world.

4. The author suggests that violence is more likely to happen when people have been reduced to a label and are no longer considered as individual human beings. When someone you know speaks of others in this way, how do you respond? If you have challenged someone to reconsider the way they box humans into a particular identity, how has that been received?

5. The author quotes Judges 21:25: "In those days there was no king in Israel; all the people did what was right in their own eyes." Do you view this as a negative statement, or can it be seen in a positive light? The author of this study suggests that the writer of Judges was making the case for the necessity of a king. What is the best sort of society that humans can form? What is the worst sort of society, as you observe it?

10

The Alternative Story of Ruth
Ruth 1–4

Personal Preparation

1. Read the book of Ruth. Reflect on the difference in climate from the book of Judges. In what ways are they similar? How are they different?
2. Consult a Bible dictionary or commentary for reflections on the date of composition and the literary genre of Ruth.
3. Prepare for singing, "Let us break bread together." If necessary, bring a digital version or sheet music.
4. Review the laws of gleaning in Leviticus 19:9-10 and care for the poor in Deuteronomy 15:7-11. How do these laws pertain to the story of Ruth?

Suggestions for Sharing and Prayer

1. Begin this last session by sharing refreshments. Reflect on what you consider the high points of this study. What learnings will you take away? Sing "Let us break bread together" as you settle into group time.
2. In what ways is the story of Ruth, set in the time of the judges, similar to and different from the other stories you have read? Reflect on Ruth's status as an outsider. Reflect on ways that your status or that of someone you know has changed from outsider to insider, or from insider to outsider. Think about ways outsiders have

made a significant impact in your congregation or in the larger community.

3. Focus on Ruth's statement in 1:16-17. How would you reword it to reflect your group's commitment to one another? Use that restatement as an emblem of your covenant study together.

4. Lift up in prayer what you have learned through this study. Thank individual members for their sharing. Gather together in a time of communion, using a loaf of bread, a large cracker, or some of the refreshments that you have shared. Sing "Let us break bread together" one more time." Close with the Lord's Prayer.

Understanding

The novel, *Ben Hur*, is set in the Roman Empire during Bible times, but it probably tells us a lot more about nineteenth-century America than first-century Judea. Similarly, the book of Ruth is set "in the days when the judges ruled" (1:1), but in some ways it tells us more about the crisis that occurred during the time of Ezra and Nehemiah when foreign marriages were banned in Israel.

The debate about the book's date of origin has not been settled. It may have been written later, but the opening declaration of the book seems to place it within the period we are discussing. Furthermore, though it is included in the third section of the Hebrew Bible known as "the Writings," when the book made its way into the Greek-speaking world, both Christian and Jews placed it after Judges to underscore its historical setting during the period of the conquest.

The story of Ruth is unlike any other story we have examined in Joshua and Judges, with one exception—the story of Rahab in Joshua 2. Both stories showcase foreign women in positive ways. In Joshua 2, a foreigner takes deliberate steps to rescue spies who would have been hopelessly trapped save for her assistance. Ruth is another story about a foreigner who rescues her Jewish mother-in-law when her own kinfolk fail to come to her rescue.

As I reflect on the tale of conquest, which opens with the story of Rahab and closes with the story of Ruth, I have come to the conclusion that those who structured our canon wanted us to consider an alternative way of acting, another way to live in a threatening environment. A Canaanite woman commits treason and risks her life to save two spies. Ruth, a Moabite, risks her life by leaving the comfort of her native family to follow her mother-in-law to Bethlehem, where Moabites are considered enemies. I shall return to why I think this story is placed where it is, but let us first examine the narrative.

The Story of Ruth

The story begins with a famine and the relocation of an Israelite family in Moab, where they are offered protection and food. Ironically, they find safe haven in a country that, in the Torah tradition, denied Israel accommodation. There, the two sons find wives. Catastrophically, the three Israelite males die, and Naomi, wife of Elimelech, decides to move back to Bethlehem where her kin reside and where food is again available. When her Moabite daughters-in-law seek to follow her, Naomi insists this is futile. She has nothing to offer them—and though it is left unspoken, they have nothing to offer her. Orpah is persuaded to remain in Moab, but Ruth refuses to abandon this widow and insists on accompanying her mother-in-law.

Naomi does not appear to be happy about this decision. When Ruth makes it clear that she will continue with her, Naomi does not say another word. In a narrative framed by dialogue, this silence is most striking. Could Naomi be thinking, "What will my clan think when I come back with a Moabite widow?" It would be like a Christian woman from the Midwest coming home with a Muslim widow dressed in a burka. Undoubtedly, suspicion would be aroused. Little wonder that Naomi does not appear to be excited about this turn of events. Her first words when she returns home to Bethlehem are: "Call me no longer Naomi, call me Mara [bitter] . . . [and] why call me Naomi [pleasant] when the LORD has dealt harshly with me, and the Almighty has brought calamity upon me?" (1:20-21). It is clear that Naomi has given up. She does not introduce or even mention Ruth.

The most famous quotation from the book occurs when Ruth says to Naomi, despite her lack of encouragement: "Do not press me to leave you or to turn back from following you! Where you go, I will go; where you lodge, I will lodge; your people shall be my people, and your God my God. Where you die, I will die—there will I be buried. May the LORD do thus and so to me, and more as well, if even death parts me from you!" (1:16-17). These words are a radical statement of commitment. Ruth declares that even death will not absolve her of her obligation to Naomi. Do not forget that in the ancient world a woman's survival was often tied to a male—her father, her husband, or her son. Ruth acts to care for a widow who has no such protection, and in so doing fulfills the essence of Hebraic law and embodies *chesed*, the divine attribute translated as "steadfast love" and "loyalty."

While Naomi abandons her faith and hope, Ruth embraces it. Ruth trusts in God when Naomi feels that God has deserted her. Ruth makes commitments when Naomi gives them up. Ruth gives up everything and embraces a new faith, a new people, and a destitute family in a foreign land. Ruth's choice is life-changing, not unlike that of Abraham and Sarah, who leave home for a destination most unclear. Ruth's choice is not for survival but for a whole new way of life. Such choices change not only the world of Ruth but the world of her mother-in-law as well.

Ruth is read in its entirety as part of the Jewish liturgy on Pentecost, the festival commemorating the revelation of the Ten Commandments on Mount Sinai. Dr. C. A. Cohen suggests there are two reasons for this. First, "the festival is . . . primarily a harvest festival and the harvest festival figures prominently in the narrative." And secondly, the Ten Commandments "marked, as it were, the formal acceptance by Israel of that religion and law of life which were later to prove so irresistibly attractive to the heathen damsel from Moab" (104). The harvest assures the continued existence of the community, just as the law assures the continued well-being of the society.

Ruth fulfills the law through obedience that transcends the letter and reaches the spirit of the commandments. She does what the law requires without ever studying it. She does not know the holy days, the laws of sacrifice, or the individual requirements. These prescriptions are not mentioned in the book. What she displays is *chesed*, covenant loyalty. This characteristic attributed to God in scripture is an active love that expects nothing in return. Ruth acts to heal a broken family and care for a widow when no one else does. In the end, she empowers the whole community to act as it should.

An Alternative Story

This narrative is an alternative to what we read in Judges and Joshua. It is also an alternative to the stories of the kings that follow. The story of Ruth is located between these two traditions—one of violence without a king and the other a cry for a king whose purpose was to restore order. The book offers an alternative history to the period of the judges, and, at the same time, demonstrates a peaceable realm without the rule of a king.

Writers such as Katharine Doob Sakenfeld contrast the escalating violence in Judges with the faithfulness shown by the women in Ruth. In Judges, the cycle of repeated disobedience against God ends with the brutal murder of a Levite's concubine by the men of Gibeah. As an example of the downward spiral and breakdown of society, the Levite divides the body into twelve parts and sends it out to the twelve tribes, inviting vengeance against the tribe of Benjamin, which is almost wiped out. To provide wives for the remaining men, additional violence and kidnapping are used to preserve the family line (Judges 19–21). Sakenfeld observes: "In the story of Ruth, the theme of preserving a family line also appears (cf. 4:4, 10), this time for lack of men rather than women. Here, however, the problem is resolved not by murder and mayhem, but through the bold and caring action of a woman . . . and the upright response of a leading male citizen who makes a moral choice to go beyond the minimum requirements of legal duty" (8). In this alternative story, the choices of ordinary people bring life out of famine and loss.

Perhaps the author of Ruth is suggesting that the choice may not be between the deteriorating situation of the judges or the strong-arm tactics of a king, nor—in answer to Ezra and Nehemiah—in putting away foreign wives and by extension outside influences, but in the choices of women and men to live according to God's law. Even though God does not seem to be acting overtly in this book, God acts through the choices of those who are obedient to the spirit of the law.

Discussion and Action

1. Do you still live where you were born? What has caused, or could cause, you to leave your homeland? Do you long for another place that you consider your real home? Are you a member of the first church you ever attended? What would cause, or has caused, you to change churches?

2. Share what you learned about the literary genre of Ruth. What difference does knowing the type of book make in the way you read and interpret it? What similarities and differences do you observe between Judges and Ruth?

3. Defining community not only as the place you live but also as the people you know or the church you share, what are the significant communities to which you belong? How do you go about choosing a community? If communities require choice, what is the difference between the choices Elimelech makes and the ones Ruth makes?

4. If you have in-laws, what have been the highs and lows of your experience? How would you describe the attachment between Naomi and her daughters-in-law?

5. Discuss the change in Ruth's status. How has your status or the status of someone you know changed from outsider to insider, or insider to outsider? Review the laws of gleaning in Leviticus 19:9-10 and care for the poor in Deuteronomy 15:7-11 (see "Personal Preparation"). What guidelines do these scriptures provide? What guidelines do your church and your community use for helping others? What limitations do you set?

6. Does your community of faith lead or follow when it comes to standing up for those on the margins, serving the poor and the hungry, advocating for prisoners and victims, or providing a place for youth? Are you more likely to embrace or avoid people who are difficult to define or serve?

7. How do you assess the initiative of Ruth, Naomi, and Boaz? When have you taken the initiative to help yourself or others? Tell stories of people who proactively made a difference for themselves or for society.

8. Ruth is, in part, a story of how an immigrant from a hated nation makes an impact on her adopted nation. In times of financial or emotional crisis, many nations—including ours—react by passing anti-immigration laws and blaming immigrants for many bad things in society. What have you heard people say about immigrants? Have you ever stood up for those on the margins of society?

Resource Pages

Prayer of St. Francis

Lord, make me an instrument of your peace.
Where there is hatred, let me bring love;
Where there is injury, pardon;
Where there is doubt, faith;
Where there is despair, hope;
Where there is darkness, light;
Where there is sadness, joy.
O Divine Master, grant that I may not
       so much seek to be consoled, as to console;
       to be understood, as to understand;
       to be loved as to love.
For it is in giving that we receive,
       it is in pardoning that we are pardoned,
       and it is in dying that we are born to eternal life. Amen.

"The Second Coming" by William Butler Yeats (1865–1939)

The poem, written in 1919 after the chaos of World War I, is a tangle of Christian and mystic imagery that reflects, at least in part, the confusion that pervaded the atmosphere of the day.

Turning and turning in the widening gyre
The falcon cannot hear the falconer;
Things fall apart; the centre cannot hold;
Mere anarchy is loosed upon the world,
The blood-dimmed tide is loosed, and everywhere
The ceremony of innocence is drowned;
The best lack all conviction, while the worst
Are full of passionate intensity.

Surely some revelation is at hand;
Surely the Second Coming is at hand.
The Second Coming! Hardly are those words out
When a vast image out of Spiritus Mundi

Troubles my sight: a waste of desert sand;
A shape with lion body and the head of a man,
A gaze blank and pitiless as the sun,
Is moving its slow thighs, while all about it
Wind shadows of the indignant desert birds.

The darkness drops again but now I know
That twenty centuries of stony sleep
Were vexed to nightmare by a rocking cradle,
And what rough beast, its hour come round at last,
Slouches towards Bethlehem to be born?

Book Review

Adapted from a review originally written for the Second Mile Curriculum.

Ethnic Conflict and Civic Life: Hindus and Muslims in India by Ashutosh Varshney. New Haven and London: Yale University Press, 2002.

There are those who think that conflict and violence are inevitable among people of different ethnic backgrounds and faith. But the book, *Ethnic Conflict and Civic Life*, suggests that people don't have to love each other—they simply have to live lives entwined together in a civil society.

The author examines the ethnic strife between Muslims and Hindus in India. The two groups have engaged in violent conflict for decades, with many dead and wounded. Some insist that violence is inevitable. But the author noticed that the violence had been largely restricted to certain cities. It rarely happened in the smaller villages. He began to compare cities with violence to cities of similar size and economics that had no history of violence. Why did some areas always burst into violence and some not, even though they had the same provocations?

What he discovered was that in villages, people of different religions and ethnic backgrounds live close together and know each other well enough that even when people try to goad them into violence they weren't willing to kill their neighbors. What he also discovered was that in the bigger cities the difference between those who broke into violence and those who did not was the level of their association in groups that mattered. In other words, in cities where people belonged to the same associations—whether unions, book clubs, athletic clubs, businesses, organizations—in which they were truly involved and shared the same goals, violence did not generally break out. People had too much in common, and too many shared interests, to kill each other.

The author discovered with further study that the same held true in the former Yugoslavia, Ireland—and the United States. When people belong to the same organizations and share daily associations they won't believe lies and will ignore provocations, and find a way to get along, even with tremendous differences.

In my experience this seems true. We lived in a racially mixed area of Los Angeles when our children were little. When the 1992 riots broke out there was violence only a few miles away from our home in neighborhoods where people did not mix, but none in the place where we lived.

This is not just an academic study. I'm convinced that in North America, and especially in the church, we need to ignore those who try to split us into different camps and divide us from each other. The church of Jesus Christ, from the first century to the present, has always included people with different politics, from different ethnic groups, and with different economic backgrounds. It should be the same now.

The violence committed by Christians against each other in our country may not usually result in fatalities, but it can be just as deadly to our ministries and missions. Among his disciples, Jesus called Galileans and Judeans, rich and poor, men and women, those with formal education and those without, blue collar and white collar workers, and even a guerilla fighter. The only thing they had in common was devotion to Jesus. It's something we should share as well.

Possible questions for discussion and action that might be asked during the study:

- What civic associations do you have with people who are substantially different from you?
- How should church members go about establishing substantial and intentional relationships with others who are quite different?
- Must associations only be among Christians, or does Christ call us to cross all boundaries and barriers?
- Why do you think that prominent people in government and media suggest we should be in a state of war, or at least wary and suspicious of those who are different from us?

Frank Ramirez

Bibliography

Boling, Robert G., and G. Ernest Wright. *Joshua*. The Anchor Bible. New York: Doubleday, 1982.

Brueggemann, Walter. *Divine Presence Amid Violence: Contextualizing the Book of Joshua*. Eugene, OR: Cascade Books, 2009.

Butler, Trent C. *Joshua*. Word Biblical Commentary. Waco: Word Books, 1983.

Butler, Trent C. *Judges*. Word Biblical Commentary. Waco: Word Books, 2009.

Campbell, Jr., Edward F. *Ruth*. The Anchor Bible. New York: Doubleday, 1975.

Cohen, A. *The Five Megiloth*. rev. ed. London and New York: Socino Press, 1984.

Davies, Eryl W. *The Immoral Bible: Approaches to Old Testament Ethics*. New York: T&T Clark International, 2010.

Matties, Gordon H. *Joshua*. Believers Church Bible Commentary. Scottdale, PA: Herald Press, 2012.

Niditch, Susan. *War in the Hebrew Bible: A Study in the Ethics of Violence*. New York: Oxford University Press, 1993.

Roop, Eugene F. *Ruth, Jonah, Esther*. Believers Church Bible Commentary. Scottdale, PA: Herald Press, 2002.

Sakenfeld, Katharine Doob. *Ruth*. Interpretation Series. Louisville, KY: John Knox Press, 1999.

Sen, Amartya. *Identity and Violence: The Illusion of Destiny*. New York: Norton, 2006.

Soggin, J. Alberto. *Judges*. The Old Testament Library. Philadelphia: Westminister Press, 1981.

Other Covenant Bible Studies

1 Corinthians: The Community Struggles . . . . .Inhauser
Abundant Living: Wellness from a
    Biblical Perspective .Rosenberger
Biblical Imagery for God . . . . .Bucher
The Chronicler . . . . .Neff/Ramirez
Covenant People . . . . .Heckman/Gibble
Country Seer, City Prophet . . . . .Neff/Ramirez
Daniel . . . . .Ramirez
Ephesians: Reconciled in Christ . . . . .Ritchey Martin
Esther . . . . .Roop
The Exile . . . . .Kline
Exodus: Freed for the Journey with God . . . . . . .Burkholder
Five Festal Scrolls . . . . .Neff/Ramirez
The Gospel of Mark . . . . .Ramirez
Hymns and Songs of the Bible . . . . .Parrott
Hebrews: Beyond Christianity 101 . . . . .Poling
The Household of God . . . . .Ramirez
In the Beginning . . . . .Kuroiwa
James: Faith in Action . . . . .Young
Jeremiah . . . . .Kinzie
Jonah: God's Global Reach . . . . .Bowser
The Life of David . . . . .Fourman
The Lord's Prayer . . . . .Rosenberger
Love and Justice . . . . .O'Diam
Many Cultures, One in Christ . . . . .Garber, ed.
Miracles of Jesus . . . . .Benedict
Mystery and Glory in John's Gospel . . . . .Fry
Parables of Matthew . . . . .Davis
Paul's Prison Letters . . . . .Bynum
Peace in Isaiah . . . . .Leiter
Presence and Power . . . . .Dell
The Prophecy of Amos and Hosea . . . . .Bucher
Psalms . . . . .J. D. Bowman
Real Families: From Patriarchs to Prime Time . . . . . .Dubble
Revelation: Hope for the World in Troubled Times . . .Lowery

Romans: Church at the Crossroads . . . . .Wiles
Sermon on the Mount . . . . .R. Bowman
Side by Side: Interpreting Dual Stories in the Bible . . .Ramirez
Spirituality of Compassion: Studies in Luke . . . .Finney/Martin
Uncovering Racism . . . . .Reid/Reid
Voices in the Book of Job . . . . .Neff
When God Calls . . . . .Jessup
Wisdom . . . . .C. Bowman

Brethren Press • 1451 Dundee Avenue • Elgin, Illinois 60120
Phone: 800-441-3712 • Fax: 800-667-8188
e-mail: brethrenpress@brethren.org
www.brethrenpress.com